middle class
nightmares

middle class nightmares

stuart holding

E&T

First published 2010 by Elliott and Thompson Limited
27 John Street, London WC1N 2BX
www.eandtbooks.com

ISBN: 978-1-9040-2792-8

9 8 7 6 5 4 3 2 1

A CIP catalogue record for this book is available from
the British Library.

Printed in the UK by CPI Group

CONTENTS

INTRODUCTION

There is no imminent risk of armed invasion to these shores; despite tabloid threats, no mass-exterminating plague stalks our land; there's very little danger of starvation to residents of the UK. As a result, members of the middle class are reduced to finding their own nightmares and horrors in their everyday lives and summoning up drama from the mundane matter of their average existences.

On asking, it has proven that this is exactly what they do, and what's more, the middle class existence as a breeding ground for the horror of social awkwardness is like a frothing petri-dish. Lots of the people in this book get themselves into terribly embarrassing situations where someone of a definitively upper or working class upbringing wouldn't bat an eyelid, but just carry on about their business. Rather than do that, our gallant heroes go straight on making things worse for themselves because they're not sure of the right thing to say (when they needn't say anything), or the right way to act (when no action at all is required).

Although a few of these tales take place outside the UK (in the Travel and Transport Nightmares chapter), all of them happen more or less within the *mis en scene* (if I can be middle class and pretentious for a moment) of the middle class life, where terrible misunderstanding and embarrassment lurk around every corner, as though we are all haunted by the ghost of Basil Fawlty.

I don't want you to get the impression this is anything more or less than a collection of anecdotes about people getting embarrassed and making idiots of themselves, because that's exactly what it is. Alongside each of the themes I've added some experiences of my own – please be assured this is not in any attempt to find meaning or conclusions from the stories of others, but only to add my own middle class nightmares to the mix.

I myself am as middle class as a Marks and Spencer jumper. So of course I'm pretty embarrassed about what I've written on the subject of embarrassment in this book – my main worry being that it's not embarrassing *enough*, in fact, which is quite confusing when I try to think about it. So, to join the twin middle class curses of awkwardness and self-deprecation, I might add that if you skip my bits and stick to other people's stories which appear in boxes, you might get a bit more out of the present volume than if you read it exhaustively.

There is also, I should add, one story that is much too terrible to be contained in the main body of the book. This story is protected by a warning at the back and I feel it's only responsible to say: do not read it if you have a sensitive disposition.

Otherwise, this book is offered humbly and for absolutely no other purpose than your amusement at the pain, discomfort and stupidity of people acting like middle class twits. I hope you enjoy it.

Stuart Holding
April 2010

FAMILY NIGHTMARES

There are two ways in which my dad has always embarrassed me when he speaks in public. The first one was the evolution of my nickname – or rather, his nickname for me, which no-one else ever used, I presume for the fact that it sounds pretty much insane.

My middle name is Roger, which is his first name. He took enormous pleasure in passing this on to one of his sons because it is, as anyone would surely admit, a horribly unappealing name. Just saying it out loud makes an unintentionally comical sound. Not many names equal it in ugliness or silliness – Derek and Nigel, perhaps, but I can't think of any others. Dad hates his name so he thought he'd make sure someone else knew what he'd been putting up with. When I was born (his fourth son), he thought it might be his last chance.

I don't mind that much because no-one has to know your middle name. Unless your dad goes around saying it in public, that is, as mine started doing when I was about 10 or 11, shouting it to me across a street, a car park or a shop.

He never actually called me "Roger," just the abbreviation "Rodge". I endured it in silence, not realising that by failing to stamp it out I was on a slippery downward slope of public humiliation.

"Rodge" quickly evolved to "Rodge Podge".

"Rodge Podge" became "Rodge Podge Diddly Odge".

I could only watch helplessly as "Rodge Podge Diddly Odge" became "Rodge Splodge".

And with a sickening certainty we finally arrived at just "Splodge".

By this stage I wasn't enduring it in silence any more. When we got back in the car after a shopping trip I would be spluttering with impotent rage. "Do you know how *stupid* you sound?" I would ask. "Do you know what you make yourself look like? What you sound like when you call me that?" He would look at me and say, "What's the matter, Splodge?" and then start the car, chuckling to himself all the way home.

Clearly my dad has no problem with looking or sounding like a fool in public. And most of the time I think that's a wonderful thing. He has no shame about having the loudest laugh in a cinema or theatre audience. When he sees someone he knows across the street he puts his hands on his hips and bellows something like, "Ah! What the hell are you doing here!" or "Isn't this past your bedtime?" and generally acts like a cross between a retired colonel and a music hall entertainer, although he is neither of those things.

Like any family we have certain sayings and stories that we are so used to saying and which are so ingrained, we forget not everyone else knows them. One of these comes from a cassette of *Hancock's Half Hour* we used to listen to as a family, which includes the episode in which Hancock and the rest of the East Cheam Dramatic Society put on a sequence of dramas. At one moment when an argument between Hancock and Sid James has broken up the action, Kenneth Williams – pretending to be a member of the audience – shouts "Get on with the PLAY!"

This became the stand-by phrase used by my parents to hurry up any one of their children (usually me) who was taking too long to tell a story (like this one), or dawdling in any way whatever. And in impatiently shouting "Get on with the play!" they would copy Kenneth Williams's archly patrician tones and generally sound incredibly posh and stupid. I lived in fear of this phrase being used outside the house because I could see that my parents had forgotten it was just a family in-joke.

So, this was the second way that my dad would embarrass me in public. One day one of my brothers was playing at the local cricket club and my dad and I were walking around the boundary. We were about a quarter of the way round, a good 50 yards from any convenient place to hide, when something halted the game for a couple of minutes, and the umpire took rather took long getting it up and running again. My dad put his hands to his mouth and bellowed in an impression of an upper-crust voice:

"GET ON WITH THE PLAY!"

Everyone turned to look at us. Everyone on the pitch. Everyone in the pavilion. People may have looked up from watering their plants in nearby gardens. No-one had any idea what the fuck he was talking about. He just sounded like a posh idiot. Ideally, right then I would have liked to be able to do the following things: firstly stop time itself. Then, sit him down and explain that these people weren't performing in a play, and that therefore (unless by an incredible statistical fluke they were all devoted fans of the complete works of Tony Hancock) they were extremely unlikely to know what he was talking about. And then hit him over the head three or four times with a cricket bat.

None of these measures were available to me right then. Not even the cricket bat. There was nowhere to go – I just had to withstand the heart palpitations of shame and embarrassment as twenty two cricketers looked on, confused, at the imbecile shouting from the boundary. My dad beamed, utterly unaware.

One sunny day I set out on a visit with my father to an open garden in the charmingly quiet village of Chipping Camden. Cue many senior citizens walking around muttering softly to one another about the hyacinths. Suddenly there was a piercing scream from my father – followed by a string of vile expletives – prompted by a bee sting to the top of his (balding) head. The disapproving looks we got were bad enough, but imagine my reaction when my father loudly and repeatedly ordered me to "suck it!" (referring to the sting, I hasten to add). Not knowing what else to do, and in full view of the oldies looking on aghast, I had to put my lips to his head and actually… suck his scalp.
E.McN.

*   *   *

I've got a plethora of brothers and a multitude of cousins. Most of these people were born long before me (owing to the various ages of my huge number of aunts and uncles aligning in a certain way) and form a clan of their own. Younger than me is another breed, numbering 20 or so, who have naturally settled into a group. The older ones show each other their babies and have dinner together; the younger ones meet up for drinks and text each other.

In between these two naturally forming groups, which have arisen from the marriages of seven aunts and seven uncles and the resulting births of 34 cousins, I was born. Surrounded as I grew up by the elder group and their bewildering sophistication, and the younger clan, many of whom were babies or as yet unborn, I had only my cousin for company.

We were roughly the same age, though he was a little older. We were fond of each other and would spend time together at formal family occasions. (In fact, despite the following story, I miss him!) Outside of this, however, we had nothing whatever in common – we were, in fact, absolute opposites. I was a nervous skinny 13-year-old who wanted to read and write. He was enormous, 15, and loved computers, code, electronic machinery and online games (when they were so new they were years shy of being cool). To pick up on the key information from the previous sentence, he really was huge. For almost my entire childhood, when you thought of him, you felt a sympathetic twinge in your own gut, for how big he was. And *every time* you saw him, he had got larger. I did love him though, with his combination of boulder-like solidity and fluttery hand-flapping when he got excited. But we didn't spend much time with each other – there was so little we could do together.

Staying over at his house when my parents were away, I was awed by the presence of a TV in his room. The night I was there coincided with a horror film season. A year and a bit older than me, his bedtime was not only later than mine but glamorously flexible and unpunishable, so long as we weren't caught on our way downstairs to fetch further supplies. And it was no ordinary horror season: we watched *Bad Taste*, the film made by a young 20-something Peter Jackson in his spare time over four years. A film in which zombies are killed by having spikes hammered down the length of their legs as they hang over the edge of a cliff, or by having chunks of their brains blown out with a gun until they are still stumbling forward with only a chin and a chunk of exposed medulla. A film so exciting, outrageous, funny and inventive that I've still not recovered from it. At 13, it positively annihilated all the previous films I'd seen. We ate snacks that were forbidden in my house and in prohibited quantities. It was a brilliant night. So this is just to explain that, at times, we really did get on, my cousin and me.

When the Flower Show came round to the local rec, we hung out together. We were too old to give a shit but too young to have anything else to do. Behind the huge marquees of show vegetables and cakes was the fairground, and we spent what money we had there. My cousin had already used up most of his cash on sweets, cakes and drinks. It was as we came round the side of the "Haunted Mansion" – so naff that no-one would ever want to go in – that we saw the spinning cage. I'm calling it that because I don't know its real name, but possibly you know the ride: you're strapped into oval cages on a ferris wheel so that as the wheel goes round, you are spun even faster on your own axis by your own weight, first forward then back, until you can't tell ground from sky and don't know where or who you are or what to expect next.

It was a scream. I screamed, certainly, with enjoyment, at being flung back over my head and then the other way in a relentless forward roll. My cousin remained silent and gripped what he could on either side of him. When we'd gone round twice, he said: "I'm going to be sick."

Immediately, he was. We were going down at the time and his vomit streamed up his face and through the roof of the cage. As we righted ourselves, I felt it spattering down on us from above. We swung for a second as the momentum caught up with the cage and he began vomiting more forcefully than before, with a growl this time, from the back of his throat, as we were spun upside down and in a jaunty swooping movement up and under the ferris wheel. We arrived a few seconds later at the top of the wheel. He was so weak he grumbled through his mouthful of puke before the momentum drove us downwards again. We could both feel that the ride wasn't quite over yet, and we were strapped in for the rest of it.

"I've got more," he grunted as we catapulted downwards. I was already screaming. Shouts and cries could be heard from other pods. I closed my eyes, heard his "blears" and "garfs" for a minute longer as I was spun upside down, and felt more splatter onto my legs, until at last the ride ceased and our iron cage was rocking gently above the ground.

People gathered round to help us out. They took him away to help him be sick some more and change his clothes but I was left to wander the fairground in a daze, until I came to, realised I wasn't presentable and had to go home. My cousin and I never spent much time together after that.

A friend of mine — a young woman in her mid-twenties — goes into to the newsagents to buy a paper with her three year-old in tow. On the way out of the shop they come to an abrupt halt; the woman in front of them has bent down to pick up some change that she has dropped.

"Mummy," the child cries, pointing, "her bottom is even bigger than yours!" And proceeds to poke the unfortunate woman's bum before her mother can catch her. By the time the woman rights herself to look around indignantly, my friend has picked her kid up, tucked her under her arm like a handbag and is crossing the street, red-faced, as fast as she can.

E.T.

*   *   *

If you're a relatively self-aware kid, one of the pains of childhood is being aware that you're in danger of saying the wrong thing at the wrong time and making adults feel extremely embarrassed, yet not knowing how to avoid it. It certainly happened to me. Wanting to impress the adults, I found myself trying to say things that sounded grown-up. Looking back, I was desperate to appear sophisticated and urbanely precocious, and to hobnob knowingly with the adults around me while my peers languished in childish idiocy. Of course I must have seemed like a weird little creep. I knew there were lots of adult things that I didn't know or understand, and I was always aware of the possibility of saying something catastrophically wrong. Like, for instance, when my mum had female friends around in the kitchen and on some random pretext I came out with the phrase: "And just when I'd waxed my bikini zone!"

I was nine or thereabout. I'd heard the phrase on some Radio 4 comedy, where it had been greeted with a laugh, and I didn't understand it whatsoever, so that meant it was sophisticated and adults would be startled and impressed at my knowing such a clever phrase.

They certainly were startled – the discomfort in the room crackled for a long second or so before someone opened their mouth to change the subject. I knew I had said something very weird and knew I would have to wait years before I discovered what it meant and cringed in horror.

My family was Catholic and one Easter we went to a retreat in the country. At this point I think I was about 11. These retreats were almost always vastly tedious and irritating, although we did have occasional breaks to explore the grounds of whatever school building or country house in which we were staying. It occurs to me now that many people might not know what a "retreat" is. I don't really remember, even though I went on many of them. It seemed to be an occasion for families from dioceses across the country to meet up with each other, talk and think about things, pray together and that sort of thing.

On the last evening of the retreat there was an evening mass to celebrate the Easter Vigil. This was interrupted by a procession where everyone went outside and the priest followed behind, carrying a huge candle through the church and into the yard, where he had to light it from a ceremonial brazier (if there can be such a thing) I managed to be almost last filtering out of the church and ended up standing right next to the priest. With a congregation of several hundred gathered watching in the cold and wind, he lowered this cumbrously tall candle to the lip of the brazier with both arms, and held it in the orange shooting flames until it should have lit. Then he lifted it up; it had not. He lowered it again.

He repeated this three times while all around people waited in silence, shuffling from foot to foot, as the evening got colder. Minutes went past as the crowd silently watched. He looked strained as he lowered it for the fourth time, then the fifth, with what I now realise was an atmosphere of sympathetic middle class embarrassment all around but which I perceived at the time as comic tension. At last he took a lighter from a man nearby in the crowd, and lit the candle close-up, to take it back into the church where it would burn during mass for the next few weeks (or something like that). I was still standing next to him, and he wearily stopped to catch his breath before going back in.

Wanting to say something encouraging and friendly (and being a creep again), I said to him, "I don't know how you managed to keep a straight face during that!" He made some kind of grudging acknowledgement, the congregation passed back into the church behind him, and the ceremony was concluded.

Later that night there was a dinner, presided over by the priest. He said grace and a few words to everyone before the start of the meal. There was a gathering of what must have been at least 200 people at the tables. Before he'd got far into the speech he made a reference to what had clearly been the maddening moment when he had tried so many times to light the candle in front of everyone. "But as I came back into the church," he told the crowd, "there was a boy who said to me: 'I don't know how you kept a straight face during that!'"

This got a big laugh from everyone in the room. I watched the reaction with uneasy pleasure, and when I had the chance I nipped over to my parents' table. "You know that 'how did you keep a straight face' thing? That was me," I said to my mum, trying to sound cool about how droll I could be.

"It wasn't!" she said, a much more forceful reaction than I expected, which put me on the back foot. She seemed amazed, but I couldn't tell for certain from her expression whether she thought me brilliant or stupid. She quickly related this to the whole table and in a second they were all looking at me.

"Was it you?" one of them asked with the same look of disbelief that I couldn't quite determine. "Really?" They all had that hungry look in their eyes as they leant towards me. I felt like I was walking on a tightrope – would they think I was brilliantly witty or was this going to become another family story about something stupid I'd done, which I'd be stuck with forever? I just couldn't tell.

"No," I said unconvincingly, which made them ask all the harder. "Yes, it was actually," I tried feigning nonchalance, and watched as their eyes widened. Whether with horror or delight, I still couldn't work out. No-one was saying anything – either to tell me off nor congratulate me.

My younger brother asked me one more time to be sure. "Was it really you?" he asked. And, at last, in my brother's eyes I saw the tell-tale gleam that he was trying to hide – he desperately wanted me to admit it. So for the first time that day I did the sensible thing. "No," I said. "Only joking. It wasn't me." And I ran off to play.

A friend of mine stands in the shower on the morning of her 24th birthday, letting the hot water wash over her. She has shampoo in her long brown hair and is not-so-quietly singing a 60s pop song.

Suddenly the glass door slides open. She squeals in surprise. Her little four-year-old daughter stands there, her expression a mixture of fear and disgust.

"What's wrong?" the woman asks, trying to wipe the shampoo out of her eyes. What can be wrong with her child?

"Mummy?" The child starts sniffling a little.

"Yes? Are you sick?" She reaches a soapy hand out to soothe her baby.

"Wheni'mtwentyfourwillmynibblesreachmybelly buttontoo?" the child rattles off tearfully.

"Slow down, sweetie, and start again," she says, still

concerned. The child wipes her nose on the clean towel on the rack.

"When I'm 24 will my nibbles [nipples] reach my belly button too?"

Thankfully the strains of Sesame Street make their way into the bathroom just at that point and the child is distracted, leaving her mother to lick her wounds and cry over her navel-bound nipples!

J.F.

* * *

I was in the passenger seat as my mum was driving along one day, when a young guy in a small car swerved in front of us quite dangerously as we exited a roundabout. My mum beeped, and with a sense of inevitability I saw the young guy hold up his middle finger to his rear-view mirror. Right up, so that the reflection was blocked by the hand.

My mum leant on the horn and kept her hand there. She was no doubt thinking, he can't expect to get away with that. Sat next to her, I was terrified – this was at the height of the "road rage" scare when every week people seemed to murder each other beside dual carriageways like this one, for no reason at all. It seemed a very short distance from here to a grave item in the local news. We were in our family estate on the way to the supermarket; he looked as though he could be on the way from an all-night poker game to dispose of a body.

She kept the horn down and did not let go for hundreds and hundreds of yards, antagonising him, until it stopped being just a noise and felt like an outward expression of my sense of alarm. I shrank as far as I physically could into my seat. I thought I saw the car in front weaving from right to left as he sought for a place to pull over. I was braced to be brutally murdered by this stranger, and yet I couldn't stop it because on another level of social awkwardness there was no way I could tell my mum what to do.

Then abruptly my mum remembered there was a short cut she could take which took us behind the library and avoided the one-way system, and she turned off the road, her temper forgotten, to continue her nice middle class existence, with me a bag of nerves in the passenger seat.

My friend Sue was at Homebase with her toddler and debating which brand of something or other to buy when she realised her son had run off. Seeking him out, she found him around the corner among the show toilets – sitting on the edge of one, with his trousers

down. Although she normally tends to lose it at the first sign of any kind of drama, this time she managed to remain calm, adjust the boy's clothes, put the loo seat down and make her way swiftly to the exit.
D.G.

RELATIONSHIP NIGHTMARES

Of course sex and dating afford such lavish and endless possibilities for nightmares – of a middle class nature or otherwise – that they're more than capable of filling a book in their own right. (Which they have done, in fact, most recently in *Bad Dates* by Sam Jordison.)

When speed dating became popular in the early 2000s it was promoted as a device that would remove the awkwardness from first dates, and introduce an element of fun into what can (for those who are prone to such feelings) quickly become a personal hell of embarrassment. And so it must have proved for many, because the practice – inexplicably as far as I can see – has continued to thrive. My suspicion is that those who are successful at speed dating are exactly the same people who have a natural knack for the old analogue version of simply asking someone out and going on a date. For people such as me, however, speed dating proved more like a sentence of hard labour than the all-expenses-paid holiday it had promised.

I was cajoled into attending a speed dating event because it was taking place opposite my office, at a chain pub which – I've taken great satisfaction in noting – has changed hands at least twice in the few years since the evening in question. One of the main reasons I (like other blokes, I suspect, who wouldn't normally go to such things) was persuaded to go along was that speed dating events are frequently advertised as being short of men so the organisers were reduced to offering free entry and even free drinks for men.

An additional benefit, I reasoned, at least in theory, of this shortage of men was that those women attending were likely to be a little bit desperate. What a relief, what a weight off, it is to be told that the ladies you're going to meet are likely to be disposed to overlook your deficits. And not only that, they might actually seek out your good points. Even see things in you that others – or you yourself – do not perceive! And ... well, damn it, don't great romances come out of the unlikeliest places? (Against my better judgement I had tanked myself up with all the optimism at my disposal, determined to ignore the fact that, really, a speed dating event is a bloody unlikely place for a good romance.) Great things, indeed, might come of it.

Unfortunately, as I said, the attractions of the event were only appealing in theory. When I got there the reality was less flattering for all concerned, and much less laden with sexual possibility. If some of the girls who go speed dating are likely to be a bit desperate, then I should have reflected that desperation is a weakness, and weakness results in defensiveness. And defensiveness tends to lead to contempt. At least it does when I'm around.

When we got there we found that although my mate Tom and I had been drafted in at the last minute, they were still short of one guy.

"That means, boys and girls," said the woman officiating, "that we'll have one poor lady who's without a date at any one time. But don't worry, because it'll only be three minutes and then you'll be onto your next lovely fella!"

She prevailed with this holiday-camp tone throughout, which put my teeth on edge. And then I discovered, as the dates started, that almost the entire quotient of females in the room were a group of policewomen who had come together. I was a rather pale and inexperienced 24; they ranged in age from 32 to about 40. Over the course of an hour and a half I met every kind of woman who works in the police, from traffic cop to morgue attendant, and I'm sorry to say they all conformed to my ungenerous expectations in that they were not of a standard of attraction that made my heart loop the loop, and that we also had absolutely zero in common. At the time, desperate to get a foot in the door of my chosen industry, I was doing a work experience placement, which led one of them to ask, with laconic disdain: "You're doing work experience? But isn't that what you do at, like, 16?" To which there is no dignified answer.

What destroyed me however was the fact that the missing man was supposed to have sat directly behind me. It was the men who moved seats each time. That meant that for every one of my "dates," the woman I had just been talking to had nothing to do but rest her chin on her hands and listen in to what I was saying to the next woman along. Without exception they did not listen in to the guy who was about to follow, who was an unknown quantity. Instead they very blatantly watched me go through a second version of my halting introductory blather, which had already been ruined by the previous woman listening in. I tried to alter it each time, make different jokes while giving across the same essential information – what my name was, what I did, what my interests were – and pretending not to notice the eavesdropper behind. I failed. I got hot-faced; I ran out of words; I wanted each date to end as soon as it started. By the end I was a wreck, and ended up talking to the only non-policewoman in there – a hopelessly twee primary school teacher from Kent – with ridiculous gratitude and enthusiasm.

When it was all over I ticked everybody on my "score card" to see who had ticked me. The primary school teacher had, but no-one else. From what she'd said, it sounded as though she still went to bed with her teddies. I didn't want to join them.

This story doesn't paint me in the best light, but here goes. I was in my early 20s and in a relationship that I knew was coming to an end — it was just a matter of time, but I was a coward and didn't know how or when I was going to break it to my girlfriend. In the meantime I'd met a girl named Caroline. I really liked her and I'd found out she fancied me too. What's more she had organised a big house party, where I knew there was a chance something would happen between us. So I had been duplicitously trying to explain to my girlfriend that I was going away to France on the day of the party (I was actually going the next day with my parents) so I could attend without her. I avoided her during the build-up to the party — if we spent the few days beforehand together it would make me feel so much worse when the Saturday came. To keep her away I pretended I'd been away visiting my parents in the country and was only popping back on the Saturday morning to pack and then go to the airport.

So when she phoned me on the Saturday morning and said she was just around the corner and coming to see me off I was thrown into a panic. Within a few minutes she was at the door and I was welcoming her in, trying to keep her attention away from the obvious evidence that I'd been in the flat for days — takeaway cartons, piles of washing up, DVDs out of their boxes. I might as well have left photos strewn over the floor of myself in the flat holding up each day's newspaper. But I seemed to get away with it, because my girlfriend was horrified to discover I hadn't started packing. The next thing I knew she was helping me pack a suitcase with all I would need for a week away in France, picking up my toothbrush, looking for my passport and so on, until rather bewilderingly I was standing in the front room ready to go, knowing that I would be back again in an hour or so. She insisted on walking me to the station, to see me off to the airport. I hadn't thought beforehand how far this could or would go but she stood next to me as I bought a ticket to Gatwick, and then came with me onto the platform and waited for the train. When it came, I kissed her goodbye and she waved at me as the train moved off. I waved back, grinning and feeling like a total idiot, and when she disappeared out of sight I finally relaxed.

The train I was on from Rickmansworth arrived at the next stop, Moor Park, and I got off, waited for the service going back the other way, and gratefully hopped on it with my bags. I sat in the window seat and stared out of the window as another train came alongside and I watched the people in the carriages until, to my absolute horror, I saw my girlfriend's face only a few feet away, level with mine. I had completely forgotten that she had to go to Moor Park to get home and that her train came back along the same line for a mile or so before it turned off towards Watford. When I saw her face, I could tell she hadn't seen me yet, so I ducked quickly under the window. I was already feeling a bit mad as a result of the day's events, so when crouching got too uncomfortable and I had to lie down on the floor, and everyone else in the carriage started looking at me, I got a bit hysterical and started laughing uncontrollably.

I waited until the neighbouring train must have long since turned off, and then sat back in my seat, still feeling quite insane. I made it to the party, got it together with Caroline and shortly afterwards broke up with my girlfriend. As I said, it doesn't paint me in the best light.

J.H.

The most mortifying experience of my life happened when I wasn't actually there. It was centred on the time my girlfriend and I lost our virginity to each other. She had a really strict dad who she was terrified of, but she'd managed to sneak me into her house lots of times before when I wasn't supposed to be there. But this was the big one, when we had planned to take the next step together. She got me in; we spent the night together; it was amazing. After a few hours of cuddling, with no-one interrupting except the family cat, we decided it was safest if I left before her parents woke up. We snuck downstairs; she let me out of the back door into the garden; I crept round the house and escaped.

I got home, let myself in and got into my own bed without being intercepted by anyone. Understandably, I was feeling quite pleased with myself. The plan had worked brilliantly. The next evening she phoned to tell me what had happened.

She had gone to sleep, equally pleased at how well our plan had gone. The next day (which was Sunday) she got up as normal and at lunchtime came down for Sunday lunch with the whole family. Halfway through the meal the cat came into the lounge and was sick on the floor in front of them. This used to happen all the time because their cat was mental and had this insatiable appetite for elastic bands. You couldn't leave them out because he'd eat them and throw them up again later — as he had just done, once again.

Sighing, her dad got up from the table, muttering something like, "Bloody cat, when is it going to stop eating those things?" Except, as he bent down, he saw that it didn't look exactly like a rubber band and as he held it up for all to see, she suddenly realised what had happened to the used condom that had apparently disappeared the night before.

J.M.

I was in the very first throes of romance with my current boyfriend of two years. I was totally in love and ridiculously keen to impress. One weekend, we were house- and dog-sitting for some friends of his. On the Saturday night, having consumed a rather large amount of champagne and not enough food, I realised that I needed to go for a poo. Up until this point, I had always managed to time the event when we were in a pub or restaurant and had never been for a number two within close proximity of him (sometimes this got quite painful). Anyway, I made my excuses and went to the loo. Once ensconced on the bog, I realised that this was situation critical, and I had no choice but to set it free.

Luckily, it was all over and done with pretty quickly so as not to raise suspicion. The handy air freshener concealed my shame even further and I was smugly pleased at my success. That is until I looked down into the toilet and saw my worst nightmare come true: a sizeable floater winking back at me. Quickly I weighed up my options. Flushing again would only draw attention to my man-sized shame and more paper would exacerbate the already dire situation. In my champagne-fuelled brain there was only one option. I picked up the offending turd (in my bare hand) and hurled it out of the window, hoping that it would be mistaken for a canine deposit. Relieved, I washed my hands and returned to my love, lady-like demeanour intact.

A.H.

After university I was temping in a lot of different jobs and I worked in this one office with a girl called Karen who was gorgeous. I was utterly besotted with her. I was so nervous that I couldn't ask her out but I managed to ask her for her personal email address, under some pretext or other. I spent the rest of the summer building up the nerve to ask her out, and after lots of encouragement from my best friends I finally made the leap. I couldn't believe it when she said yes, and I planned various ways to make the date as brilliant as possible. I got us tickets to a band who I remembered she said she liked (what with everything she'd ever said in my presence being burned on my mind and all), worked out the best bars to go to and so on. When I went to pick her up from her parents' house, she unexpectedly invited me in. There were some uncles and aunts over for dinner, and quite a party atmosphere. I said hello and generally tried to act as cool as possible. Then there came a sort of shouting from the back of the house and I wondered what was going on. I'm not sure how to put this with absolute political correctness, but a boy came into the room who was clearly mentally disabled. He was trying to get his parents to come and look at something, and his relatives, and us too — he wouldn't be placated until we all came along.

As we filed into the back room my date, looking decidedly uneasy, tried to explain what was going on. She told me that the boy was her adopted brother and owing to the fact that he had a weird list of foods that were the only things he would eat, he was massively constipated and only did a dump about once every three weeks. When he did do one he was inordinately proud, and would insist on showing everyone.

"Insist?" I laughed. "What if you don't want to go?"

She stared at me. "You don't understand, Steve, he insists and won't let up until you look at it. And I mean everyone – you included."

I was still getting my head around this when his aunt and uncle came out of the toilet in front of me, making loud comments of congratulation and saying "Clever boy!"

The next thing I knew I was in there and actually staring down into the toilet bowl. The turd was unbelievably massive. It was about the size of a Gideon's Bible. I stared at it for slightly too long. Then I was face to face with him, looking into his expectant eyes. Unbelievably I managed to do it: "That's great," I said, "it's amazing. Well done." And then I was allowed out.

As we walked to the gig she explained that it was always like that when he "went". I asked whether they were always so incredibly huge and she admitted that they were – in fact, they could hardly ever be flushed down, she added, and quite often the family had to dig them out of the toilet and bury them in the back garden.

There was nothing I could do about it; the magic was gone forever, replaced by the image of that unbelievable turd. We watched the band, had a quiet drink afterwards, and never spoke again.

S.H.

The other night I drunkenly stayed over at my ex-boyfriend's. In the flat that he shares with a friend, all the rooms lead off the hallway. My ex has an ensuite bathroom but his flatmate, someone who I'd never particularly got on with, doesn't. In the morning my ex left at about 4am to go skiing, but told me to just stay in bed and get up when I normally would. Waking up a few hours later, I started getting dressed and gathering my things together, when I suddenly heard a loud blast of Take That from the flatmate's room. He obviously thought he was alone in the flat, having heard my ex leave several hours earlier, and was merrily wandering

from bathroom to bedroom fully naked, singing along to "Beautiful World" as he got ready for work. There was no way that I could sneak out without him seeing me and I genuinely considered hiding in the bedroom until he'd left. However, given that I had to be at work in 45 minutes, that wasn't a viable option. In the end I took a deep breath, opened the door, shouted "Hi!" and ran out, to his screams of shock and embarrassment.
L.H.

During my second year at university, a couple of friends got together after a long "will they, won't they" period. Some months later, the relationship was going really well and they'd met each other's parents once or twice. During the holidays, James was invited round for lunch one weekend. Like most of us, he was somewhat intimidated by Amy's mother, who was generally considered terrifying and who didn't seem desperately keen on him when they'd met previously. Naturally he wanted them to approve of him and as a result, by the time the date came round, he was already feeling anxious.

He arrived on time at their house and rang the

doorbell. The house had quite a small doorway and inside there was a step going down, as the floor was set slightly lower than the ground outside. Amy's mother answered the door, which threw him off a little more. She began to lean in towards James as she said hello and he realised that she was intending to greet him with a kiss on the cheek. But he wasn't sure which way he should go and the two of them got locked into one of those really awkward dances where they both moved their heads the same way each time. Desperate to put an end to the embarrassing scene, James decided he had to be decisive, pick one side and stick to it. He took a stride forward down onto the step, stuck his head out firmly – and somehow found himself with her nose wedged into his mouth.

They both jerked apart and there was an excruciating moment of silence. Then Amy's dad, who was standing behind his wife, stepped forward and said "Hello!" rather heartily. No-one said a word about what had just happened, which made it even worse, and James had to sit through the rest of his visit replaying the scene over and over in his head.

C.S.

*   *   *

If you've discovered nothing else so far, you know there's

a kind of joy to hearing someone else's horrible stories. As the French novelist Michel Houellebecq (who is unquestionably too highbrow to be referenced here) has said, finding out about another person's misery can really put a spring in your step.

So, although it seemed completely unfunny to me at the time, you may find some enjoyment in the story of the most embarrassing moment of my whole life.

I went to university in Bournemouth and in my first year stayed in the "student village". The single window to my room was totally overhung by the surrounding walls and admitted no light. And it rained constantly – I don't have a single memory of it not raining during the whole winter. Across the rain-swept car park, I could see the pointed building which housed all the extra-curricular services: the doctor's surgery, yoga classes, a chapel, the piano room. The piano room was at the front of the building, a broad glass-fronted hall with a grand piano in the centre, by the window. It appealed to my sense of self-dramatisation that I could play the piano and be noticed by passing girls. I had enjoyed playing the piano when I was younger, and had only given up learning because of the usual teenage shiftlessness. I searched through the notice boards, found that piano lessons were available and signed up for them. I wanted to learn one brilliant, impressive piece of music, something which would be really fun to practise and play in a large hall. My teacher recommended Rachmaninoff's *Prelude in C Sharp Minor*, a crashing and obnoxiously loud performance piece.

I practised day after day in that large hall, happy to be away from my unpleasant student house, as rain hammered and slanted across the windows next to me. Many girls walked past as I crashed out the dramatic ten-finger chords with all their majestic force, but none of them stopped or said hello, or watched, or gave any sign of giving half a shit what I was up to. After a while I realised that there was a very pretty girl who had her lessons after me. It seemed to me that she was just about in my league, though at the absolute top of it.

The end-of-year exams came round. I had spotted the girl was in the one of the same modules as me; we had an exam coming up, which fell on piano lesson day. Being in her presence always made me incredibly nervous and over the course of several months I hadn't managed to say anything more to her than hello. But now I had a chance to help her out – when I got to my lesson the week preceding the exam, I told the teacher about it and that neither of us would be able to attend lessons. As the girl hadn't mentioned it herself, the teacher and I decided to move both lessons to another day. I only had to let her know this had happened.

I'm still not sure what exactly prevented me catching up with the girl. It may have been the fact that I knew nothing about her, we had no mutual friends and I had basically no way of making contact. Or I could have been drunk the whole week. Either way, I failed to pass on the message. The exam came and went, and the next week I was in my piano lesson with my very nice teacher, a lovely and slightly hippy-ish blonde woman of about 40. Still a few minutes from the end of my lesson, there was a quick knock on the door and in stepped the girl, as beautiful as ever. I was delighted to see her, until I noticed she looked quite tense.

The teacher finished playing a phrase, then stopped when she saw that the girl had come into the room. From the girl's expression I suddenly realised that this was about to go wrong, and there was nothing I could do about it.

"Are you ... Stuart?" she asked dubiously.

"Yes," I said. "Hi."

"Did you ..." she checked herself, as though she couldn't believe she was about to make such a weird accusation. "Did you," she persevered, looking supremely doubtful, "... change my piano lesson last week?"

"Yes," I began. "I'm sorry."

All of a sudden, in the expression on her face, I could see just how weird that made me look. I decided to try to explain.

"Yes," I said, "I'm so sorry. I knew you did the same module and I knew we had our exam, so you would miss your lesson ..."

She stared at me in confusion.

"But my exam wasn't last Wednesday," she said, "we did it on Thursday." She was clearly totally baffled. It was becoming apparent that my attempt to do her a favour had hugely underlined the fact that I had no part in her life – in her eyes, I'd singled myself out as the very archetype of a meddling outsider.

"I just don't understand why you did it," she said for the second or third time. It began to seem like this was never going to end, because I was never going to admit I'd done it in order to snog her.

I'd said sorry about 15 times by now, and the word didn't have any meaning any more. I was mumbling down at the keys and the teacher was sitting beside me, unable to do anything but watch.

Receiving neither protest nor adequate explanation, the girl peered at me as she tried to understand why this had happened to her. "I was revising all day and I had to stop and walk for half an hour to get here," she said, "only to find my lesson was cancelled, changed by you. Then I had to walk back. I missed more than an hour of revision!"

It's really horrible to be in a situation where, if you were to witness it yourself, you would definitely take sides with the other person. By now, I was reduced to making pleading faces. But the girl (as gorgeous as ever) was baffled, standing there with her anger still unappeased. She had one final point to make emphatically:

"But I don't even know you," the girl protested loudly. "Who *are* you?"

I was still stuck on the piano stool, with the teacher sympathetically mute next to me. I didn't have a response, except to repeat what I'd said before, that I was trying to help and got it wrong, and was really, really sorry.

This had taken up the last couple of minutes of my lesson, and hers was now due to start. I had to struggle out from the piano stool with as much dignity as I could, which – red-faced and weak-kneed – was none at all. Then I had to gather my stuff, put it in my bag, thank the teacher and walk out. The incredulous stare of the girl I had fancied for much of the year followed me all the way out of the room.

*　　*　　*

Once, at university, I got utterly, completely stoned with some friends – so mashed that it felt like an epic undertaking to stand up. Sooner or later the film we were watching came to an end and someone switched off the telly. One of my friends managed to leave, meaning the only other two people in the room were a couple who I knew well.

Equally stoned, they began cuddling and kissing and (there was nothing else to watch in the room) I began to get quite embarrassed by the spectacle. They saw that I was unable to move and so started kissing more and more passionately to try and embarrass me. And they succeeded – I felt incredibly awkward, as that's the last thing I wanted to intrude on. But I was so stoned I couldn't bear to move, and just had to sit there getting more and more embarrassed.

After simulating it for a while, they began to get massively into each other for real and because I was silently sitting on the floor and they were still mashed, they forgot I was there. Like a coma victim, I watched with a growing sense of horror until the moment when she pulled his boxers off, which was the shock I needed to get up and stumble out of the door, albeit in slow motion. When I got back to my own room down the corridor I was unsure whether they'd been winding me up or not, but was still hugely embarrassed. So I phoned them up to apologise for interrupting them shagging. And it was only when one of them answered that I realised that I was interrupting them all over again. Even though they could see it was me calling, I hung up.

O.T.

My friend — a teenage girl — gets off the train at a major station. She is meeting an old friend, whom she has recently discovered to be the love of her life. People are milling around everywhere and she is quite short, but she can spot his green football jersey and red hair anywhere.

"Okay," she tells herself, "I'll just do it. He has to find out some time. And who knows? Maybe he'll feel the same way." She steels her nerves and sets off at a brisk pace before she has time to change her mind.

When she reaches him she throws her arms around the 6ft tall man, shuts her eyes out of fear, and plants a kiss on his lips. To her great relief, he dips her and gives her the most passionate kiss in return. Some people around even cheer the young couple.

Coming up for air, she breathes, "I didn't think you liked me like that." To which he answers, in a strong American accent, "I know exactly what you mean." Her eyes fly open and she looks at him for the first time.

From somewhere else she hears the voice that belongs to her true love calling out, "Sarah? What are you doing?" In front of her are two red-headed men. Both clad in green football jerseys with blue jeans. "Nice shirt," says the boy she's come to see.

"Right back at you, dude," the American replies, grinning broadly, "and it's very nice to meet you," he says, holding his hand out to shake Sarah's.

M.W.

During sixth form I was going out with a boy called Rob, and we went in for all the soppy stuff in a big way – making mix tapes and buying stupid cards for each other. I have absolutely no musical talent and while most people can put together a collection of songs that go together, my approach was more along the lines of "well we've had a slow song now, let's put in a fast one next." Needless to say, because it was from me, Rob loved it. One evening his parents had a big garden party, and someone told Rob (as the youngest sibling and therefore the one with the best music taste) to go and put on some music. He went and got my tape, put it on the tape player and pressed play. Before too long, his three older siblings started ridiculing him – saying things along the lines of "God what is this? Rob, I thought you were meant to know something about music! Ha, this is rubbish! Seriously, are you deaf or something?"

I stayed quiet, hideously embarrassed but safe in the knowledge that no one knew this was my work – until the eldest brother went to get the tape out of the player and announced to the group: "Oh it's got a label on it! Let's have a look... 'To Rob, from Sophie'..."

It's hard to say who was more mortified.

And a sequel...

In my first year at uni, Rob and I went to Hong Kong with his family for the rugby sevens. Which was fine, except that no-one knew that we had actually broken up a couple of weeks before, and Rob had persuaded me to come on the trip as a last ditch make-or-break holiday. Deep down I knew it was a mistake and a few days later, while on a night out, Rob and I had an argument and I broke up with him for good. To my horror, Rob started crying in the bar and his (extremely over-protective, except where mix tapes were concerned) elder siblings immediately stormed over to find out what had happened. On learning that I'd just dumped their darling younger brother, they told me I was selfish and immature and refused to talk to me for the rest of the holiday (another eight days). This would have been just about bearable had we not been staying at a family friend's house, where space was at a premium because of the rugby, which meant that we five were all sharing a bedroom. Even worse, three days before we left, I developed a dry, hacking cough that no amount of cough medicine would help, so every night I lay there in a room full of people who hated me, coughing incessantly and keeping them all awake.

S.P.

About a year ago, I met a guy I liked while out with some friends. We got on really well so we exchanged numbers and arranged to go for a drink the following week. By complete coincidence we bumped into an old school friend of mine in the bar we were in, and when my date went to the loo she came over for a gossip. I told her that the date was going terribly — whatever chemistry had been present when we first met was now most definitely gone, and we were well on our way to exhausting the usual tired uni/travelling/work anecdotes. She was quite drunk and told me not to worry and to leave it to her to get me out of it.

When my date came back from the loo he suggested we take our drinks outside as it was a really nice evening. An hour or so later, when the date had hit rock bottom and there were lengthy ten-minute pauses between each of our conversations, something caught my eye and I turned round to see my friend pressed up against the window, eyes closed, simulating getting off with the glass in a particularly raunchy manner. My date turned round to see what had caught my attention and we both watched in silence as, still with her eyes closed, she writhed against the window. "And you... know her?" he asked. Date over.

M.H.

A friend of mine had just started seeing her new boyfriend when she went to go and stay with his parents during the university holidays. His parents were quite conservative and made sure that she slept downstairs on the sofa in the lounge. Obviously they kept making excuses about needing to do some "revision" and heading upstairs. During one particularly energetic session, they managed to break his bed – the single bed he'd had since childhood. Panicking, they constructed some long-winded tale about Jo sitting on the bed and Sam jumping on to say hello, and went downstairs to confess to his parents. The entire family came back upstairs to survey the damage and it was only then that Jo realised that, in their panic, they'd forgotten to remove the used condom from the bedside table.

C.H.

The other night I met a guy on a night out and we started talking. Quite drunk and wanting to impress, when he told me that he was in the army I told him that I was also really into exercise and fitness, despite that being completely untrue. "Really?" he asked. "Whereabouts do you run?"

Lacking inspiration, but thinking on my feet, I reeled off a route that basically went round the Northern line and thus included Clapham Common, London Bridge and King's Cross.

"Really?" he said. "But that's about fifteen miles!"

"Yes," I finished lamely, "yes, I run fifteen miles every weekend..."

E.M.

I was in a club during my first year of university, standing on the balcony with my mate Steve, when I spotted a girl at the bar below. She was truly beautiful and appeared to have no-one to talk to, that I could see. Steve said I should go down; I said no, I'd only fuck it up. This was the dynamic of our friendship – Steve was successful with girls (insofar as he could actually talk to them and also went out with them) and I wasn't (because I couldn't and didn't). This struck Steve as the moment to finally give me the pep talk I needed. He inflated my ego; he told me how easy it was just to talk to someone, and be yourself and that there was nothing stopping me doing it; he told me I'd have a great time and it would go brilliantly. He filled my nervous head full of dreams, sent me down onto the dance floor and watched me as I walked around the three long sides of the balcony, then down the stairs and across the floor to the girl.

When I reached her I stood stupidly in front of her for a few seconds until she noticed me and then, totally unable to start a sentence, I blurted out over the music:

"HELLO! CAN I HAVE YOUR PHONE NUMBER?"

She looked a bit confused, and said, "Er, no, I don't really just give my phone number to strangers."

"Okay!" I shouted. Then I stayed put, not knowing what to do, for seventeen seconds. I counted. Above me, Steve must have been watching, thinking "God, he's actually doing it, he's having a conversation with her. This is going brilliantly!" In reality I was just standing there next to her, with no expression on my face.

Finally I couldn't stay there any more and turned away, shouting "OKAY, BYE!" I walked away from her as fast as I could in a straight line through the smoke-machine-filled dance floor, only to see the smoke parting too late. I walked full-face into the wall. I bounced off painfully and had to pretend not to notice the girl, now surrounded by friends, watching me. I then had to walk back across to the stairs and up and all the way round the balcony again to re-join the incredulous Steve.

T.W.

WORK NIGHTMARES

My greatest work-related embarrassing story – and when I say greatest I mean most epic, most David Lean-like – was to do with the sick bay.

It occurred during a period of what could only be described as intense boozing. I had been going for drinks with a girl I knew from the office almost every night and was edging closer with each passing evening to getting her into bed. I had only been working at the company for a short while and it was my first proper job, so I was still living with my parents out in the sticks before moving into London. This meant that in the course of any evening's drinking, as 11 p.m. drew closer and then arrived, the danger increased exponentially. And with it, so did the attractiveness of just one more drink.

On this particular night, as we both drank more, I became convinced that the moment had finally come. Various admiring remarks and a general shift towards a more yielding attitude made me increasingly confident that it was going to happen. 11 p.m. arrived and we left our usual pub to visit a sequence of progressively more dingy late-night places. Eleven-thirty came and, as we had new drinks, I made it clear that this meant I was going to miss my last train home.

She seemed philosophical about this. "You can always sleep in the sick bay at work," she said, with a knowing smile. I laughed. In the back of my head, I knew that until 12.30 a.m. I could still get a tube to Vauxhall, connect with the 1 a.m. train and get a ten quid taxi at the other end, so I hadn't burned all my bridges, only the convenient ones. Half-twelve came; we were still getting on famously; half-twelve went.

By 2 a.m. we were being kicked out of the last bar still open in King's Cross. Emboldened by the lack of rejection so far, I tried to make it clear that, with no other option, I'd have to stay at hers.

"I don't have a spare bed," she said.

"Well," I said.

"I don't have a sofa. I don't have a living room. There is literally nowhere in my flat that you could sleep except my bed."

"Well," I said.

"And that's not going to happen."

Unfortunately I didn't avail myself of the opportunity to take this like a man. In truth, I felt like I'd been led most of the way up the garden path and a certain wheedling quality entered my voice. "I wouldn't try anything, for God's sake. Of course not!"

"That's right, you wouldn't, because it's not happening," she said easily, as her 24-hour night bus lumbered noisily alongside. "I told you: you can sleep in the sick bay at work. The building's open all night."

I wrestled with this as the doors hissed shut and she waved goodbye. No matter how I tried to reason it (and I didn't have much else to do at nearly 3 a.m. in King's Cross, except smoke a few cigarettes) I couldn't help feeling a bit disappointed. In fact, the more I reflected upon it, being led up the garden path seemed a bitter understatement. I had long ago passed from the garden path in through the French doors, been handed a large G&T, regaled with hilarious tales over roasted pheasant and been invited back the next week for a spot of tennis.

Refusing to give in to the humiliation of sleeping at work, I paced the streets for about half an hour, positive that there must be an alternative. I knew dozens of people in London, including two of my brothers. Surely there was a way out?

At that point my phone rang. It was the girl. She said sorry for treating me badly, that she did in fact like me; she thought something could happen between us, and she hadn't meant to leave me abandoned like that in the street. I was speechless. If there was one thing I hadn't seen coming at this point, it was the situation suddenly going in my favour again. In fact, I started to see how funny it was that I'd been made to sweat it out so hard before this point.

"So I can stay at yours!" I said. "Where do you live?"

"No," she said sadly, "I don't think it would be right."

It was at this point that I lost my temper. At the top of my voice I made it clear how I felt about the situation I was in, her involvement in it and how that reflected on her in general, and hung up. I walked around the block a few times in a blowing gale, like a kind of young King Lear, and, as the alcohol wore off, realised that I was exhausted. I had to be at work in about five hours. The risk of being caught sleeping at work had become much less frightening, and seeing as I couldn't go home and take the next day off sick, the idea of catching five hours sleep was basically an imperative.

At the security door I mumbled to the guard that I knew how late it was, but I had to come in to fetch something. I had a working security pass so he had no choice but to let me in, and I went down into the basement to the sick bay. When I finally set eyes on the bed, I couldn't think why I had hesitated to come straight here. Although it was only a rudimentary cot no larger than a camp bed, now, at four-thirty in the morning after seven hours' drinking, it looked like an earthly vision of paradise.

I turned the light out, shed my outer garments, shoes and socks and stowed them invisibly underneath the cot. Then I opened a large bottle of sparkling water that happened to be standing by the bed and drank from it, set the alarm on my phone, pulled the sheets right over my head so that I wouldn't catch the eye of anyone walking past the glass panel in the door, and fell asleep.

What followed felt like about six minutes of blissful slumber. It was interrupted by a brief and hazily remembered shouting match with the security guard. His suspicions finally aroused after I had been in the building for several hours, he had hunted through every floor until he found me and when he did he stood in the doorway yelling incredulously that I had to get out. I shouted back that I had every right to be there, had no intention of going anywhere and why didn't he bugger off and leave me alone, and finally won the argument by falling back asleep.

I was woken by my phone's alarm at 8.15 a.m. The office's opening time was 9.30 a.m. There was a lot of booze and tiredness still in my system so instead of thinking, "Thank God I woke up in time – now I can freshen up and be at my desk when other people come in!" I thought, "One of the only benefits of sleeping at work *has* to be that you don't have to set your alarm so early ..." I switched it off and fell back asleep.

The next thing I knew the door crashed open, the light was switched on and a trolley was shoved to the bedside. Now I was certainly awake, and knew that this had suddenly gone terribly wrong. Leaning right over the bed was the enormous lady who stocked the meeting rooms in the building. That's why there'd been a bottle of sparkling water here – all the supplies for the building were kept here and she had the Thursday acquisitions meeting to prepare for. She was reaching over to grab bottles from the other side of the bed, two at a time, and her eyes were practically looking into mine but she wasn't seeing me because she didn't expect me to be there. I pulled the cover right over my nose and watched her, my eyes swivelling from side to side, with growing terror. What would happen when she realised I was there? Would she scream and run out? Surely she'd make a complaint about me either way? How many health and safety or behavioural codes was I infringing by being in her work space and nearly naked? It was going to happen any second now. She couldn't keep staring at me and not see me!

At last I saw it register with her that someone was in the bed – she froze and let out an astonished theatrical gasp. I had no idea what to do (apart from ignore my first instinct which was to say, "Please don't scream") so, feeling as though I was in some kind of pantomime, I simply raised my finger to my lips and did a conspiratorial "Sshhh ..." as though I was trying to remain hidden in a game of hide and seek.

She stared at me, then nodded slowly, placed the last two bottles on the trolley and wheeled it back out as quietly as she could, turning the light off behind her. I lay there in the darkness for a while wondering if I could get another fifteen mintues' sleep, then decided that was probably pushing the risk factor a bit too far, and got up. I snuck into the showers and eventually reached my desk, more or less on time but knackered, and feeling completely and utterly absurd.

Interviewing people is dull. Lacking the bowel-loosening frisson of being interviewed yourself, the candidates you meet quickly fade into a kind of beige uniformity and as interviewers you find yourself saying to each other afterwards, "That one with the hair, you remember ... No, the other one."

On this day, however, there was Lucy. Lucy was quite something. In fact, she had been a finalist for Miss South Africa a few years before. Suddenly my co-interviewer woke up and started leading the charge with all manner of questions he hadn't thought to ask the previous incumbents of the blue swivel chair. With his full-beam smile and awkward, overly frequent running-of-hands-through-hair, he could not have been more transparent.

The end of the interview arrived and Lucy had demonstrated she was as overqualified for the generic admin role we were trying to fill as any of the other candidates we'd seen that day. To wrap it up, my co-interviewer said, "Well, we've got other people to see yet, but – you know – you're an incredibly beautiful candidate."

Which was inappropriate enough, without him following it up with a five-minute attempt to explain that he had meant to say "credible candidate" and a plea to the baffled but indulgent Lucy not to sue him or the firm for discrimination.

M.S.

My friend Craig used to work at a very staid insurance company and one day, during one of his many frequent but short-lived health kicks, he bought a pot of natural yoghurt for lunch. Deciding he didn't want to eat it then after all, he put it in his desk drawer. A few days later, having forgotten all about it, he opened the drawer to find that the live bacteria in the yoghurt had caused the pot to explode and there was now yoghurt all over his drawer. Craig being Craig, he simply shut the drawer, forgot about it again and a few days later went off on holiday. He came back to work two weeks later and walked jauntily into the office, only to find out that his desk had completely disappeared. Slightly bemused, he made some enquiries, and it transpired that in his absence, a colleague had opened his drawer

to get something and a huge swarm of flies had flown out. The desk had to be completely destroyed and Craig was given a health and safety warning.
R.S.

*　　*　　*

I've mentioned elsewhere that in my mid-20s I did quite a lot of work experience for various companies in an effort to get my first proper job. It is not only a tried and tested route to getting permanent employment but often seems like just about the only way in – when I finally did get a job, I discovered my boss had got his break exactly the same way 15 years before. I bring this up because being in the position of doing work experience gives multiple and varied opportunities for being embarrassed or humiliated, depending on your aptitude for ending up such a position (which for me is high) and also on the inclination of the people in charge of you for making you feel that way (at times, also quite high).

Once I'd got my job after all the work experience, I still managed to get myself in trouble when I started going out with a young woman (a graduate, I should point out, by which I mean she wasn't sixteen) who was herself doing some work experience in my current place of employment. The fact that she was on a work experience placement and I had been looking after her made us both a little unsure about the potentially exploitative nature of the relationship, and it became a running joke between us that "this" was what I did with "all the work experience girls". By playing along with the joke, I made the idea seem totally out of the question without actually denying it per se.

Soon my girlfriend and I found ourselves at the birthday party of an old friend of mine who had not met her yet. My friend, George (a girl), was delighted to meet my new girlfriend and made the usual kind of friendly chit-chat asking where she was from, what did she do, how had we met, and so on. This brought the conversation round to the fact that we had met through work while she was doing some work experience for me.

"Oh really?" asked George, giving me a semi-beady glance.

"Yes," said my girlfriend. "Of course I'm worried that he always seduces the work experience girls, ha ha!"

I don't know if you've ever had this feeling, but I suddenly realised that I couldn't change the conversation, and had the vertiginous feeling of knowing I was about to get rumbled and there was nothing I could do about it.

"Oh, not all of them," said George, smiling, "it's only happened once before." Totally fair enough, she assumed that I'd been honest with my girlfriend (which I would have been eventually, I just hadn't felt the moment was right yet), but I received an intensely icy stare from my girlfriend and George looked mortified at having stuck me in it. The relationship didn't last very long after that.

> I was temping as a PA for a large advertising agency in central London. I was new to the job and didn't really know what I was doing. My then boss, who I "looked after," asked me to sort out his travel from Liverpool to Euston for the next day. Now: a) I'd only just moved down to London from South Shields and at that point I wasn't aware Euston station even existed, so b) I presumed he was talking about Houston, Texas. Why exactly I thought this is still not clear to me as I had his schedule for that week in front of me and I knew full well it did not include a one-day visit to America.
>
> But I called the company travel agent, who seemed a tad confused, and got prices for travel from Liverpool John Lennon airport to Houston airport. I emailed the details and itinerary to my boss and his "team," which included around ten executives. There were a few sniggers around the office and eventually one of the execs came up to me and quietly said: "He means from Liverpool to Euston Railway Station, London."
>
> I was mortified. I wasn't asked to book his travel

again and was not invited back to work for them the following week.

R.T.

Darren is a successful lawyer who has been to many banqueting dinners in his time. But, years ago, he had to attend his first such occasion. As a fresh-faced graduate surrounded by his elders and betters, he was determined to keep his head down, get through it and scarper as soon as he could. He negotiated the starter successfully and then came the shellfish course. A great many unusual implements and bowls were laid out before him and then a steaming mass of crab, lobster and langoustine was placed in front. To stop himself from panicking, he simply decided to copy the rather odd-looking woman sitting to his right. Being a well-raised middle class boy, he was determined not to leave an empty plate, so on he troughed.

Once the course was finally done, he looked down the table to his left and saw a line of bowls filled with discarded claws and legs. But not his own – or his neighbour's. He had chomped his way through every single shell. He managed to make it to the toilets just in time.

M.S.

*   *   *

The prime humiliation of work experience is that (unless you're a pushy pain in the arse, in which case they can't wait to get you out of the door) you have to totally accept your "nobody" status, while wanting the chance to do the stuff that the people all around you are doing. At one point I spent two weeks at a very successful publishing house, where in one afternoon I managed first to humiliate myself and then be humiliated by the people around me.

I had spent most of the two weeks I'd been there silently filing their prodigious collection of publicity clippings about their books, which for some reason (like no-one else wanting to do it) had been gathering on top of filing cabinets for quite a while. I hadn't learned much except that I didn't like the junior publicists, who generally gave off an air of chilly disdain, and that I didn't particularly want to work for them. However I had recently given up my job as a bookseller and was relying on my parents to support me while I tried to find work, so when on my second last day one of the more senior publicists came over to thank me for the work I'd done, I was very grateful for the chance to talk to her.

"I really appreciate all the hard work you've been doing for the last few weeks," she said, "we're very grateful. What are you doing next? Where are you hoping to work?"

I realised that this was the only chance I had to impress someone who might actually make the effort to help me out; that my two weeks' effort had all been in order to get this opportunity. I blathered on about how much I'd loved working as a bookseller, but that I wanted more of a challenge, and wanted to see if there was a chance that publishing might be for me ...

For some weird reason at the time I had a bad habit of scrunching my toes fiercely when I was nervous but wanted to appear calm. Maybe this is similar to the way that other people bite the inside of their lip or dig their fingernails into their palms, I don't know, but my way of maintaining a controlled exterior was to scrunch my toes up very tight, almost till they hurt.

I finished making my nervous and rambling speech to the senior publicist and she began wishing me good luck in getting a job and saying that she was more than happy to take me along to the editorial department to see if there were any tasks they could give me to do. Still furiously crunching my toes, I had forgotten that one of my toenails was ripped. All of a sudden another toe caught on the loose one and tore the nail almost completely off. While the kindly female publicist was in the middle of her speech, my face suddenly twisted with a grimace of pure agony. I quickly got over it and forced myself to look normal again, but it must have looked as though I was either deliberately trying to freak her out or that I had a ghastly facial tic. As she was mid-sentence and already being nice to me, there was no polite way for either of us to bring it up. Instead she walked me down the length of the floor to the editorial department, no doubt a little bit frightened and hugely relieved to be rid of me. I limped behind, and remorseful shame made my skin crawl.

This meant I arrived in the editorial section slightly out of sorts, disconcerted and in a bit of pain. As the publicist handed me over, I found myself in a room of about 12 people working quietly and was introduced to a young man who looked rather slick and pleased with himself.

"Hi," he said, smiling blandly, "nice to meet you. So you're interested in editorial work? Tell you what; could you be so good as to look at these for me?" He pointed at a pile of manuscripts in his in-tray. An afternoon spent reading book submissions? Yes, after weeks of ceaseless filing, I could definitely do that. I went to take them off his desk but the girl sat at the next desk along suddenly burst out with a loud voice: "You can't get him to read your SLUSH PILE! That's so insulting!"

"No, really," I said, as quietly as I could. "It's no problem. I'd like to do it."

She was one of those girls who beam all the time, even when they're saying something really horrible. She didn't pay me any attention and carried on shouting at her work mate. "You're so RUDE! You can't get work experience people to do that!"

Muttering that it was absolutely fine, I retreated to my

desk where I got through the two armfuls of submissions in half an hour. It was immediately apparent that the books were all utterly unsuitable for publication. I returned to the guy's desk and handed them back, telling him so.

"Thanks," he said, smiling wanly again, "er, I think my colleague has some work for you to do." He pointed to the girl who had leapt so vociferously to my defence earlier. As she saw me she gave me an oh-it's-so-sweet-of-you beam.

"Hiyaah!" she bellowed, and pointed to a teetering pile of paper on the corner of her desk. "I was wondering if you could help me out with some submissions ..."

*　　*　　*

I don't know if this story is "nightmarish" enough, but hopefully I can get across how much of a terrible person it made me feel. I work for a renewable energy charity in London, and I'd not been there for very long when one day I was clocking off for lunch in a particularly good mood. I can't remember why (and to be honest, after this, I've not really felt the same way again). We have a storage cupboard where we leave all our bags, but what with most employees being young and active and into healthy things, it doubled as a changing room for when some of my female colleagues did lunchtime yoga or Pilates in one of the empty offices.

I'd received emails about not going in there at certain times and saying to look out for the sign on the handle, but I hadn't really paid attention. Anyway, as I say, I was in a good mood and as I reached the kitchen I saw one of my new colleagues, who struck me as a nice guy, coming the other way. He said, "Hey man!" in a really upbeat way and in response (I can't tell you how out of character this is) I did that really corny thing where you pretend to use you hands as guns and shoot the other guy, while saying, "Heyyy!"

Just as I was finishing this smarminess, I reached the storeroom and marched straight in to grab my bag only to hear a voice behind me squeak, "Excuse me! Trying to get changed here!" I stopped in my tracks, totally trapped. Apologising profusely, I had to manoeuvre myself back out of the door without turning round and seeing my naked female colleague, which I managed with a lot of bumbling clumsiness and further apologies. I finally got out of the door and forlornly looked at the sign on the handle – it did indeed say "Do Not Disturb" but in really small writing, and both sides of the sign were exactly the same colour. What's more, as I slunk away, my mojo well and truly destroyed, I realised how it must have looked to my male colleague – that I had been full of beans because I was happily bounding over to the store cupboard to get a good gawp at/sexually harass one of the women in my new workplace.

H.M.

At the end of the day at work, a male colleague (who happened to be French) and I were going to an evening event. Before we left the office, he needed to go to the gents so I waited for him outside.

As he stood at the urinal, he could hear somebody huffing, yelping and more or less crying out from one of the cubicles, and from the noise it sounded like it was due to some constipation-related injury or pain. Just then, our senior manager came into the toilet, saw my friend at the urinals and said hello. The noises stopped at once, the cubicle dweller now suffering horribly in silence with the senior manager bliss-fully unaware.

As my colleague left the cubicle and joined me on

the stairs he struggled to explain what had just happened. He was trying to tell me about the man in the cubicle but his English wasn't so good, and after frustratedly trying to explain for a minute or so he asked me what the English word is for *urinoir*. Quite oblivious to what had happened, I told him loudly and clearly that it was "urinal". He then noticed that the senior manager was just behind us on the stairs and as it seemed weird and unprofessional for us to be discussing the man in the cubicle, he shushed me.

The second he did that he realised it must have seemed like he had been going to say something about our senior manager standing at the urinal, and there was no way of making it sound any different. We all walked in silence to the event.

J.D.

A friend of mine had a final interview for a job he desperately wanted. The interview was with the MD and three other senior associates, so he was quite nervous. Fortunately, it went really well and he got up to leave at the end feeling extremely relieved. Unfortunately, the interview room had two doors side by side; one was the exit and the other was the door to a cupboard. My friend stood up, shook hands with each member of the panel, walked confidently over to the door and left, only to realise he'd walked into the cupboard. Panicking, he didn't know what to do so he stayed put, despite the fact that all four members of the interviewing panel knew he was in there, until finally the MD knocked on the door to ask if he was alright.

E.U.

PARTY NIGHTMARES

I always, always look forward to parties. In anticipation, I love them; they live up to my every dream. The other guests are funny and attractive, I'm funny and attractive, the music is a mixture of favourite songs and great new discoveries, I get pleasantly drunk but not out of control, and it goes on until we stagger out with the beginnings of dawn on the horizon, to find a night bus waiting nearby which takes us home to a warm bed and, in the morning, only enjoyable fuzziness instead of an actual hangover.

In practice, of course, they're almost uniformly loathsome. I've always been in the habit of blaming myself for not being good at talking to new people, but as I get older I'm not sure it's entirely my fault that conversations falter. The more people I meet, the more I begin to suspect that other human beings in general just aren't that interesting. Maybe it's simply that your chances of meeting interesting people at a party are really quite low. And once you've ruled out the chances of connecting with anyone there on some rudimentary human level, of course the possibilities for humiliation multiply exponentially, like bacteria.

The purest kind of middle class nightmare is one where you humiliate yourself thoroughly with no input from anyone else at all. Just you, on your own, making the situation work to your disfavour. Just such a tale is the following one.

This happened (as with several other tales I've included) while I was an unpaid intern at a London book publishers in the summer of 2005. Already a very successful company, over the course of the ten weeks I was in the publicity department, it celebrated an astonishing run of near-continuous number one bestsellers by its major authors. On each occasion, several crates of champagne were ferried into the boardroom and at the end of the day the whole company left their desks to come and raise a glass. (I obviously wasn't being paid so would hang around with whoever stayed on and drink as much as I could, with the bizarre result that after a few months there as an unpaid intern I was impoverished and yet actually sick of champagne. Although I did manage subsequently to regain my taste for it.)

The author we were toasting on the day in question had actually been in the office a few weeks before, on the day of the 7/7 bombings, and had ingratiated herself to the generally terrified and traumatised staff by marching around self-importantly and asking loud rhetorical questions about how she was going to get home. Nevertheless, here she was a few weeks later at the number one slot with everyone gathered around hiding their resentment behind raised champagne glasses.

As usual I was acting as waiter at the party, partly because it's a good way to suck up to important people you barely know and partly because I do actually think I'm rather good at opening bottles of champagne – I can do it so it makes a barely perceptible *oomp* noise. I was in the middle of this operation, with foil and wire top removed and finding the cork harder to twist than usual, when someone started tapping a glass. The room hushed down and everyone seemed to turn to look in my direction. I realised that the author, who was quite short, was standing right in front of me, so it felt like this whole successful publishing house was staring at me in silent expectation, just as I was about to open a bottle of champagne.

Having just been doing my best to yank it open, it suddenly became imperative that I keep the cork in the bottle so as not to detract from her speech. As she began to speak, I pressed the cork back in with all my strength. This was late July and the boardroom had skylights, which were admitting strong shafts of sunshine. I pressed the cork until my wrist began to ache and the skin on the ball of my thumb was indented into the shape of it. Come what may I was not going to screw this up and become "that guy who hilariously fucked up that author's speech".

Straight away I began to sweat profusely. A mixture of alcohol, heat, stress and physical exertion made for the perfect combination. Within seconds the sweat streamed from my forehead and all down my face, while I tried to maintain a kind of rictus grin in spite of the pain shooting up my arm. Meanwhile, the author was giving a "thank you" speech that was quite passive aggressive – she actually finished with the words, "Now you've got me to number one, you'll have to do it again next time!"

I think I sweated about a pint in what can't have been much more than three minutes. As the speeches ended everyone clapped and I finally, cautiously, took the weight off the cork (I have an acute fear of champagne corks going off unexpectedly, even when it's not in a potentially career-threatening situation). Holding the bottle up carefully in front of me, I discovered that there was no risk of the cork coming out at all. In fact, now that people were once again milling around, and I needed to return to my waiting duties, it became clear that I was holding an implausibly well-tempered bottle of champagne. After wriggling it around as I tried to keep the pressure on for nearly five minutes, it showed no sign of coming out. In fact despite my best efforts, spurred on by increasing anger, I found it almost impossible to open.

There were other bottles popping all around me and glasses being filled, and what's more I was sweating again as I struggled with the bottle once more. I refused to give up, moved away to an uninhabited corner of the room and twisted and yanked with all my might until the cork finally came out. The half of the cork that was inside the bottle was straight, not a champagne cork at all, and the wine in the bottle was still, even though the label was identical to that on all of the other bottles of champagne and the bottle had the wire and foil-capped top.

Completely drenched with sweat, I put the bottle down and with what small amount of dignity remained to me, accepted a glass of champagne from someone else, drank it, drank another, and withdrew from the party.

This took place about eight years ago, when my wife, Sara, and I had been going out for about a year but I hadn't yet met many members of her family, as they lived in Ireland. The exception was her younger sister, who lived in London and who we'd been out with a handful of times. I found her a bit hard work to be honest, as she somehow always managed to piss Sara off in some small way each time they spent an evening together, so I was already wary of her. It was a family event — someone's birthday, I think — and my brothers and parents were meeting several of Sara's siblings, who happened to be in London, for the first time. We went to a pub in Clapham and for half an hour or so Sara and I were standing next to each other near the bar, talking to my younger brother. Then Sara turned round to talk to one of her sisters. I carried on chatting to my brother and a few minutes later, finding Sara was quite close to me, I affectionately put my hand on her bum. Absent-mindedly, I ran my fingers back and forth across her backside for a good 30 seconds before I realised it wasn't her. I yelped at the top of my voice and jumped. Her younger sister had been standing there frozen to the spot all along, too terrified to move as I carried on feeling her up. In my defence, they're the same height and colouring, they had identical-looking haircuts and that night they were wearing similar outfits.

Luckily my wife thought it was hilarious, because she liked to see her sister and me both made un-comfortable. Relations with the sister-in-law — never warm — cooled slightly, which was fine by me. The trouble was neither woman changed their haircut so I was pretty embarrassed when, a year later, I made the same mistake again. My sister-in-law and I don't really speak now.

F.G.

My brother Henry and I were at a party the other day when this girl came up to him, gave him a massive hug and started talking away. We all assumed that Henry knew her but when she went to go and get a refill, it transpired out that he had absolutely no idea who the girl was. In due course she came back and started talking away again, before stopping, turning to us and saying, "Oh, you must think I'm so rude, Henry hasn't introduced me!" She then paused, clearly waiting for him to step in and do the necessary introductions. There followed an awkward pause before she realised that Henry wasn't going to say anything. "What's wrong, Henry?" she asked. "It's almost like you've forgotten my name!" More awkward silence – at this point, the rest of us wanted to die while Henry laughed uncomfortably and said, "No, no … you don't need me to introduce you!" She finally twigged what was going on and demanded, "Henry, what is my name? Tell me what my name is!" At which point Henry had to admit that he had absolutely no idea who she was, and she threw her glass of wine in his face.

E.M.

I was back home in the Midlands for Christmas a few years ago and went out drinking with my brother. I go out a lot in London but I'm not a big drinker, and I tend to sip one drink for most of the night. But it was Christmas Eve, I hadn't seen my brother for a few months, and we kept running into old schoolmates in the pub, so I forgot myself and matched him pint for pint. After midnight a group of us were staggering home down a dark lane, meandering from one side of the road to the other, my brother leading the group back to ours to open a bottle of whiskey and keep the night going in my parents' kitchen.

Blackout.

I woke on Christmas Day feeling awful. There was definitely a chunk of the end of the evening that I couldn't remember and something about it made me feel terrible – not just gut-wrenchingly ill, which I certainly was, but sick because I was sure I'd done something bad. Gradually, as I managed to sit up and look around my room, it came to me that I must have thrown up somewhere. But where? I couldn't bear not knowing so I started searching everywhere – under the covers, under the bed, in the chest of the drawers, under every moveable object in the room, behind the curtains, everywhere I could think. Tentatively I went out of my bedroom and began to look in embarrassing places — the laundry basket, the kitchen cupboards, behind the settee ...

Meanwhile everyone was carrying on around me like nothing was wrong, so I tottered cautiously back to my room and sat on my bed again, wondering if maybe it wasn't true and the distant memory of vomiting in the dead of night was just a bad dream. After all, I told myself, I'd looked everywhere it could possibly have happened. I mean, everywhere! Except, obviously, the cupboard by my bed, where I'd hidden all my wrapped presents the night before ... Slowly I got up, walked to the cupboard and pulled the door open. The scene that confronted me was utter carnage.

S.B.

A friend of a friend of mine was at a dinner party at a very swanky house that belonged to an acquaintance of his. The host was rich enough to have his own wine cellar and made a big deal out of it with various remarks (such as how he had only reminded himself just in time to bring the red wine up the night before or else it wouldn't have risen to room temperature naturally, and so on and so forth). Obviously this made his guests (none of whom had their own wine cellar) slightly resentful, and just then his wife called him out to the kitchen to help with the first course.

After he'd gone, one of the guests leant over to take the current bottle – which was white – out of its holder and have a look at it. He hadn't heard of the vineyard and didn't know much about the region either, but as he was going to put it back he saw a small handwritten label, about the size of a price tag, on the back of the bottle. Squinting, he read, "crap wine, serve very cold". He showed the guest next to him, who passed it on in turn until it had gone all the way round the table and had been placed back in the holder just before the host made his re-entrance to the room, which now had a slightly charged atmosphere. There was no obvious way for the guests to get their revenge, however, and so they ate the food and continued their rather stiff conversations, and it began to feel as though nothing was going to be said and they would have to go home with the host having suffered no comeback for his arrogance. That was, until the end of the first course when the guest who had noticed the bottle in the first place conspicuously

sniffed his wine glass, took a dubious sip and said loudly: "May I say, this wine complements your wife's cooking perfectly."
A.D.

I went to a dinner party recently and was slightly ill at ease. I don't particularly like them at the best of times – deep down everyone knows that they're just false occasions which encourage you to act more like a wanker than you really are, right? Anyway, I got promoted last year and found myself being in charge of people for the first time, which wasn't a position I had really intended to end up in, and then (as a consequence) I was invited to dinner by one of my employees. It was perfectly pleasant, the people were friendly and interesting and gradually I began to relax into the experience. I don't normally drink much but I'd had a glass of wine (which was delicious) to help me along and was so relieved that the evening was going better than expected that I became a bit garrulous.

A bit later on into the meal, the husband of my

employee reached over to the red wine decanter, which was now empty, and asked if anyone wanted any more wine.

"If you've got any more of that stuff," I said, with uncharacteristic enthusiasm, "then yes! It's absolutely beautiful." He looked a little confused and I wondered how such an effusive compliment could have caused offence. "That was the one you brought," he said suspiciously.

Unfortunately the wine, as I said, had made me garrulous, and instead of laughing this off I tried to explain it. "Ah, oh, yes," I said. "You see, er, we don't normally drink much red wine. And a friend came round a few weeks ago and brought that and, er, I knew we wouldn't get round to drinking it, so I brought it ..." There was a chilly pause around the table as I realised that, quite early on in the evening, I'd managed to make myself seem both rude and tight. My fear and dislike of dinner parties – for a moment overcome – was firmly reinforced.

J.V.

This might seem like an urban myth to you, but it genuinely happened to someone I know.

My friend Ian had only recently gone to university and was having a very heavy party season in the lead-up to Christmas. It was halfway through the night at something like his fifth or sixth piss-up in a row, getting reasonably drunk and talking to some girls he didn't know, when he suddenly realised that he was so wrecked with all the drinking over the past week that he had uncontrollably fouled himself.

I don't know if you've ever done that yourself – I suspect that lots of people have but no-one talks about it, for obvious reasons. Anyway, if it should happen to you and you are in company, the instant you realise what's happened you've got about ten seconds to get out of the room before the smell becomes an unavoidable talking point. So Ian desperately made his excuses and pushed through the crowd to the toilet.

Once inside, he stripped down, cleaned himself up as well as he could and put his clothes back on – except for his underpants, which were the only soiled garment and totally beyond repair. In fact, as he looked himself up and down, he was really rather pleased with how well he had got away with it. The only question was what to do with his pants. The toilet and the bin were both definitely out, so the only answer he had was to open the window and fling them into the garden. He yanked open the window and chucked them out, then exited the bathroom, rejoined the party and congratulated himself on avoiding a potentially disastrous situation.

It was only as he was on his way home afterwards, and telling the story to me, that he realised that he had been wearing pants into which his mother had sewed a tag with his full name on it.

B.D.

My friend Liz was invited to a childhood friend's twenty-first birthday party. The dress code was "Tropical" so of course she turned up clad in Hawaiian skirt and coconut bra, only to find that the rest of the guests had interpreted it slightly more conservatively and were all wearing floor-length green Prada with the odd feathered earring. Knowing no one, she inevitably hit the red wine rather hard and when dinner had finished and everyone was on the dance floor, she realised that no one had sung "Happy Birthday" to her friend. Convinced that this would make her friend's night complete, she stumbled to the DJ booth and asked to borrow the mic. She then launched into a very loud, slurred version of "Happy Birthday" while the assembled guests stared at her. Not only did no one join in but a couple of people actually started booing her, and halfway through the song she realised that the DJ had switched the mic off in pity. She left soon after.

E.M.

After a fairly drunken BBQ at a friend's, at about 3am my friend James said he was going to head home in a cab. James and I have been friends for many years, and have often crashed at one another's flats in the past, so drunken logic dictated that it would make more sense for me to go with James back to his parents' house (in Richmond) rather than get my own cab home (to Old Street). We got back to his, and after sharing another ill-advised bottle of wine in the kitchen, headed up to bed. This was the first time I'd been to James's parents' house, so a little while later, when I needed the loo, I woke James up to ask how I got there. He sleepily mumbled some directions to me and off I went. I made it to the loo absolutely fine, but when I came out, I was faced with a long corridor full of identical-looking doors – and, by this time being very drunk, I had absolutely no idea which one I'd come from. After wandering up and down the corridor for several minutes, growing increasingly more panicked, I decided that I had to pick a door because the alternative was to just sleep in the corridor and that would be odd. Unfortunately, but slightly predictably, the door I chose was James's parents' bedroom. His mother woke up immediately but to her credit, did not act at all surprised to find a strange drunk girl wandering round the house looking for James's room in the middle of the night and instead calmly directed me to the right door. Conversation around the breakfast table the next morning was somewhat stilted.

A.B.

A few years ago when I was a mere scrap of a lad in my early twenties I decided to go out for drinks in London with some mates from uni. Going out for drinks in London was quite a commitment, as my bedroom was on the other side of Essex and my journey home nigh-on impossible after 10pm. It was, therefore, with heavy heart and drunken head that I foolishly agreed to stay on my friend's floor. Foolish because one of his flatmates was an alchololic ... who didn't like drinking alone.

I awoke the following morning feeling dreadful. Paralytically dreadful. Luckily my working day didn't start until 11am and so, as I was a few tube stops away from my workplace, I could lie in. On the floor. In an unpleasant-smelling sleeping bag. After closing my eyes for what I thought was 10 minutes but what actually turned out to be 3 hours, I awoke with unbearable nausea. Leaping to my feet I ran to the bathroom ... only to remember that I had no idea where the bathroom was. You see, despite having spent a good few hours in the flat mere hours ago, the combination of deadly booze I had imbibed had left my memory a little fuzzy.

As everyone else in the place had taken themselves to work, I decided that a madcap sprint into every room was the only way I was going to be able to dispose of this vomit acceptably. I burst into the kitchen, the front room, the flatmates' bedrooms (one I accidently went into twice in my panic), but finally found the lavatory. This relief, coupled with my overwhelming 'unsettled stomach', caused what could only be described as a vomit volcano to explode from my mouth into the tiled bathroom. It went everywhere. I crumpled to the ground, dragged my way over to the toilet and proceeded to empty my guts vocally into the bowl. This was not yet my lowest ebb. When the waves of illness had subsided I decided to, after a brief (somewhat involuntary) nap on the cooling porcelain, try and clean the bathroom. This was how I found myself in my boxer shorts, a grotty damp sponge in one hand and a pint of water in the other, sitting on my friend's lavatory wiping my sick up and down his once clean tiles. Stopping occasionally to vomit some more. This, still, was not yet my lowest ebb.

After performing the worst excuse for a scrub-down in the history of cleaning I was somehow able to get myself upright, dressed and ready to leave. I had packed my sleeping bag into its impossibly small holder (a feat that caused sweating, swearing and a little mouth vom) and had made it to the door. I walked out into the hottest day of the year (not an exaggeration, it genuinely was the hottest day in that year) and contemplated a small kip against his front gate. Regardless, I summoned all of my strength and made for the tube station. On the way I stocked up on Lucozade, water and, for reasons I still don't understand, a Milky Way. I was feeling slightly better. Upright. Human. I would get to work, have a well-deserved cup of tea and make it through the day. I sat on the tube carriage thinking everything was going to be alright ... only to have my stomach disagree violently as the train lurched forward.

Going to work at 12:20 had its benefits on this particular day, the primary one being the lack of innocent bystanders having to witness a pallid, sweating gentleman accidently projectile vomit a curious concoction of Lucozade, water and Milky Way across the railway carriage he had sat down in moments before. In my defence, if such a thing is defendable, I genuinely thought I was just doing a little cough, not a lottle sick. I was ashamed, but this was still not yet my lowest ebb.

I stood and headed for the door. All I needed was some fresh air and everything would be alright. The train pulled slowly into the station – my sanctuary – when I saw her. The lovely, pretty, excited girl who looked as if she was out to chase her dreams in our nation's capital. Now, I am not a religious man, but I'm not ashamed to admit that I prayed genuine prayers that the door I was standing opposite would not somehow align with her blameless, unsuspecting self. But stop it did. My stomach tightened and, whilst the tinny beeps indicating the imminent opening of train doors sounded, I vomited onto the glass in front of this unlucky, undeserving traveller's face. She looked startled as I broke past, mumbling apologies, and ran towards the next victim of my excess – the station cleaner.

The following few seconds were a blur. I remember grabbing the garbage receptacle from the cleaner's hands with force. I remember the clear plastic slowly filling with a less clear liquid as my head sank into it. I remember more mumbled apologies as I ran for the exit. I remember falling against a wall and sliding down on my back. I remember reaching into my bag and cleaning the sick from my face with the first thing that came to hand – the dirty sock I had been wearing throughout the previous day. And I remember knowing, at that precise moment, that THAT was my lowest ebb.

The remainder of the day was far less eventful. I managed, somehow, to make it to work, to commute home and, somewhat improbably, to go to the pub that evening. The following day I decided to ring Alex (my uni pal) and apologise for the utter shambles I was. He, as always, laughed it off with gentle good humour. In fact, he mentioned, the only person who was a little bit pissed off was his other flatmate, who wanted to know why there was a small piece of onion hanging from the bristles of his toothbrush ...

J.M.

On our fifteenth wedding anniversary my husband and I were booked to go to a fancy restaurant, to forget the daily grind for an evening and just eat out in style for once. Of course, having three children under the age of 12 didn't help and, no matter how much we'd looked forward to the evening from a distance, by the time it came round I was so tired and stressed I wasn't really looking forward to it at all. The babysitter was late and George was putting our middle one (who was being a pain) back to bed for the third time. All ready to go, I found myself giving the kitchen a sweep and wiping down the surfaces while I waited for him to come back down. Eventually he did, just as the babysitter got there, and we finally got out of the house – both exhausted and not in the mood for a "proper" evening out. As we got in the taxi my clothes felt a bit uncomfortable but I didn't really notice, and when we got to the restaurant the maitre d' was decidedly off with me. By then I didn't care. I just wanted the evening to be over so I could go to bed.

As we stood at the bar to order some drinks first, I noticed three pointed looks in a row from different ladies around me. I started to feel cross – I knew I looked out of place but I didn't like being made to feel more so. Then I had a moment of awful paranoia. I looked down and realised I was still wearing my apron. I moved right up against my husband so that no-one could see, and whispered furiously into his ear.

"Why didn't you tell me I was wearing this?" I asked. He looked down my front as though he didn't know what I was talking about. "Wearing what?" he said. "That? I thought it was part of your outfit."

H.R.

After the dullest wedding ever in the Outer Hebrides, my husband and I decided we'd stop in Edinburgh to catch some of the festival. Finding a cheap hotel was impossible so our only option was to stay in the Ritzy 5* Balmoral – a seriously opulent hotel.

After checking in, the relief from being away from boring family members meant a large drinking session ensued. After taking in a few pubs around Edinburgh, we headed back to the hotel and carried on drinking in the bar. Finally shattered, we passed out and went to sleep.

This is where it gets really embarrassing. I must have got up in the middle of the night to use the bathroom, but I was still asleep. In my somnambulistic state, and disorientated due to my unfamiliar surroundings, I apparently walked out of our hotel room wearing nothing but a pair of pants. Yep, I then proceeded to walk around this massive – and I'm talking *massive* – hotel in the nude.

I woke up standing in a stairwell. It took me a moment to work out where I was, at which point I realised I was in the middle of my worst nightmare. Of course I couldn't remember our room number and was completely freaking out at this point. In the end I decided, modesty aside, I had no choice but to find a security camera and jump up and down (despite being sans clothing on my top half).

To cut a long story short, eventually I found my way out of the stairwell and came across a porter. I had to stand there talking to him, covering my boobs and explaining that I couldn't remember my hotel room number and could he please look it up. They eventually led me back to my room and let me in, where I found my husband completely fast asleep and unaware of my nocturnal wanderings.

J.H.

TRAVEL AND TRANSPORT NIGHTMARES

I arrived in India with my mate Kev, as naïve as could be. Neither of us had ever been outside Europe before, but here we were setting off on a round-the-world-tour. We had bought Lonely Planet guides for each of the countries we were visiting, but as a result of our relatively pampered upbringings we were so accustomed to having everything done for (or explained to) us that it didn't seriously occur to us that we might need to do any real research beforehand. Loads of people did this round-the-world trip thing all the time who seemed stupider than us, and they seemed to get by alright. So we would too, surely?

The flight from Gatwick to New Delhi was truly incredible. When we weren't marvelling at the fact that this was all finally happening, we were looking out of the window at sunrise over the Himalayas, or snoozing. We had split the various guidebooks between us. It was when we got to New Delhi, and stepped into a vastly empty arrivals lounge bags in hand, and Kev turned to me to ask what we did next, that I got to perform my long-rehearsed gag. I sat down on a nearby bench, pulled the guidebook from my bag, theatrically turned over the first few leaves until I got to the introduction, looked up at Kevin and read: "India. It's impossible to encapsulate this unwieldy combination of cultures ..."

Kevin laughed. It was a good joke. The idea of two completely ignorant people arriving in one of the most vast and complicated countries in the world and knowing literally nothing about the place was funny to both of us. I felt quite pleased with myself. Then it wore off and we were both still there, bags in hand, with no idea what to do next. We were supposed to be in India for four weeks. I didn't much like reading guidebooks and genuinely hadn't thought beyond that sight gag, just presuming we would wing it.

What followed was a week of pretty much unrelieved confusion and misery. The second we stepped outside the arrivals lounge we discovered why it was £100 cheaper to travel after 1 May – because we were in the sweltering furnace of an Indian summer. You could buy bottled water but by the time you got back to your hotel room it was blood temperature, and didn't feel refreshing at all.

We suffered the attentions of a sequence of taxi drivers who over-complicated our simple little tourist lives. We knew from the book that there was one particular street where most tourists stayed. But no matter how often and loudly we insisted on being taken there, we were driven to hotels where we were welcomed and booked into a room before we knew what was going on. Naturally we were overcharged for everything we did in these hotels and our expensive progress towards the genuine travellers' centre of New Delhi was a sequence of arguments where two pale and polite south London boys gradually discovered how much of a temper they had to lose.

On the second day we found our way to New Delhi's main mosque. We were assailed through the cab window by adorable-looking children but tried to ignore them, knowing that giving them money would make it worse. On the steps of the mosque, however, we hesitated over where to leave our shoes. A sharply dressed young man darted over and showed us where to put them. Then, with quick nervousness and energy, he asked if he could take us round the mosque. Kevin wasn't bothered either way but I said yes, happy to have a personal guide to this great monument. In a couple of minutes we had passed round the main square of the mosque, had the various sections pointed out and been given a very brief account of its (no doubt fascinating) history.

"You can put your shoes on now," said the lad at the gate.

"Okay, thanks," I said dubiously, feeling that it was

a slightly more abbreviated guide than I had expected. Then I realised why I had placed such trust in him: he looked and acted exactly like a young Martin Scorsese. But an Indian version. The second I realised this I couldn't take my eyes off him. He was hanging around us in a totally unrelaxed way as we put our shoes on, as though he didn't want to ask us for money but wanted to say something. Looking up from tying my laces, I asked him how much he usually got for his "tour". He said 500 rupees. That was a hell of a lot for us – a whole day's budget, at least – but not wanting to make a scene at the door of one of the greatest and most sacred places of worship in the country, I paid up. He saw my pained expression as I handed the money over and he asked if I felt it wasn't a fair price. We'd been screwed by enough people by now for me to be honest.

"No," I said, into his innocent, Scorsese-like face, "I don't think it was worth it." He looked terribly unhappy. I felt that I had somehow cheapened his religion by being there and giving him the chance to fleece us.

The mutual misery between us and the city's inhabitants didn't end there. If you're being fleeced by professionals, at least the relationship's quite clean. Afterwards, you all know where you stand and if you're the victim you can put it down to experience and write it off. If everyone involved appears rather amateurish and you manage to make your fleecer feel bad in the process, it somehow makes you feel even more unhappy about the whole experience. And this is what happened again, soon after.

This time we were determined, no matter what, to find the main travellers' street, where we could meet others and get some decent advice. The previous night, exhausted, roasting hot and very pissed off, we'd paid a taxi driver to take us to what he said was the only off-licence in the city (and he didn't seem to be lying, we never saw another) where we got a small bottle of whisky and two litres of coke. Returning to our over-priced hotel, we searched the channels on our telly until we found something in English – *The Fifth Element*. Neither of us had ever enjoyed a Hollywood film more than in that hotel room, giddy with dehydration and drunkenness, smoking cigarettes and revelling in the excessive nonsense of the culture we'd left behind. The following morning, emerging from our hotel with the familiar feeling of being hung-over, we felt better able to deal with our exotic surroundings in a grimly unforgiving fashion, and get to the travellers' district.

The poor driver who picked us up was a shyster of the lowest and least competent order. He was a paunchy man in a grubby white suit, with the hopeless eyes of someone who feels things are constantly slipping out of his grasp. He had the usual taxi-driver's level of English insofar as he would listen to where we wanted to go, nod and then promise to take us to his "brother's" hotel, which was "very good". We lost patience with him extremely rapidly. He drove for five minutes and then left us by the side of the street while he dived into a hotel to see whether they would give him a cut for delivering us to them. They were clearly full because he reappeared looking slightly put-upon and drove us on, saying he would take us to his brother's hotel, where we would be treated very well. At the second one he was turned away again, and came back to the cab looking positively deflated.

He began to drive us to a third hotel but we had already been shouting at him constantly for about half an hour by then. We knew that New Delhi was not New Mexico or Tokyo, and if we were already in the centre we could not be a 40-minute drive from the very central street where we had ordered him to take us. As he drove to the third hotel, it started pouring with rain and when he muttered an excuse to us and dived in through the front door, we grabbed our bags and followed him out onto the street, screaming the name of the street we wanted to be taken to. He flapped desperately, telling us this was his brother's hotel and it was very good, and we finally vented our feelings about brothers' hotels in general and his in particular, called him a liar and said we had no intention of paying anything for the long taxi ride that had taken us nowhere. We left him looking soaked and utterly hopeless – pathetic in both senses of the word – on the street corner. Looking back, his main crime was that he wasn't as good a liar as the other taxi drivers, who utterly ruined the first few days of our trip by holing us up at places we couldn't afford (and screwed with our budget for the rest of our holiday in the process). But because he was more inept than they were, he received all our pent-up, middle class anger and I've always felt bad about that.

The second time I made a New Delhi resident regret trying to get money out of me was about 48 hours later, when Kev and I had decided (without much trouble) that we were having about as horrible a time as was possible and we had to move on as soon as we could. We found our way to the railway station, where we were determined to get the date of our departure brought forward. We trailed from one office to another, being offered dispiritingly unclear advice as to what we should do and what documentation we needed. Within minutes we'd picked up a trail of people offering advice, rogue tickets and translation services, as well as the beggars and mad people who seemed to gather there. Kev walked at a furious pace from one office to another in the hope of getting our tickets changed and getting out of there as fast as possible, while I felt increasingly ill and lagged behind.

We marched up some stairs as a group of jabbering people kept pace with us. Kev got to the top and looked back as I leant against a pillar. I waved him on like a character in a war film, as if to say "Go on, save yourself." The importunate locals gathered around me with their insistent voices, offers and advice, and this helped bring my situation to a head. Looking upwards, my head swirled for a second and then I bent forward and was sick on the floor in front of them all. No words in my middle class vocabulary could have done the trick as well – they were gone in a second, and I lent back with giddy relief, protected from further intrusion by the pool of puke in front of me.

Eventually I started to feel better and Kev came back to find me. Within 24 hours we were on our way out of the city on the unexpectedly and thrillingly efficient Indian rail service.

I was on the tube last year and a man got up to let a "pregnant" woman sit down. But it was that moment that everyone dreads on public transport because what he didn't realise (though it was obvious to everyone else on the carriage) was that she wasn't pregnant, just fat. As he stood up and moved out of her way, he saw everyone was looking at him in a funny way. He looked back at the woman, now seated, and then at us, and said in a disbelieving voice, "What, is she not pregnant?" Everyone in that carriage cringed and died a bit inside. I stuck my head back in the book I was reading and after a while we realised that, thank God, the woman had her iPod on, so hadn't heard his remark.

O.H.

This happened to a friend of mine. He was on the crowded underground platform at Oxford Circus. A packed train stood waiting, possibly with just enough room for one skinny person to squeeze on but no more. Unfortunately a robust lady carrying huge bags was so miffed that she couldn't fit into the space – despite a few good shoves and heaves – that she stood braced, like a forward ready to take out a nippy fly-half, stopping anyone else from boarding the train. A small crowd of tutting people clustered round, knowing that it was some minutes until the next packed tube would arrive, but she would not budge.

Eventually Gil decided to make a move. He slid his slight frame between the woman's bags and the doors and clambered into the vacant space. She fumed silently in his general direction. The doors closed. Gil gave the woman a beaming smile, raised both hands to his ears, waved them about in a nuh-nuh-ne-naah-nuh fashion, puffed out his cheeks in a subtle nod to her big-boned aspect and blew a raspberry. After a jolt, the doors slid open again and the two of them stood silently, nose to nose, for two full minutes before the train finally left.
M.S.

*   *   *

I have no memory of the next story, which comes from my friend Diana, although I was the main character in it.

After our arduous journey through India, Kev and I had landed up in Singapore. Following on from the mess of Mumbai, Singapore's pedantic neatness looked totally un-human and cartoon-like, so we were happy to move north to Thailand to relax for a few weeks on one of the cheaper holiday-oriented islands. A couple of days in we were amazed to find out via email that a girl we knew from school – the only other person we knew who was travelling at the same time – was also heading to Thailand and wanted to join us for a few days.

Before we knew it, Diana had arrived and we were having a drink, smoking a joint and generally having a good time. She had been teaching in Kathmandu and told us how cross she was to have reached the end of her stay without once getting food poisoning, which was guaranteed to lose you a stone in a couple of days (not that she needed to, I should add). She had even taken to eating ice-creams from street vendors, which were notoriously dangerous, to no avail.

Now she was here, she decided to stay with us – in fact, as each hut at our beachside encampment had a double bed and therefore charged for two people, we said she could bunk down in the same rather huge bed as us for a few days.

The first night, after some utterly delicious food in

the open-air dining area with the other residents, we got very stoned with them and drank plenty of beer and local spirits (whose name I can't remember, maybe because they were unscientifically distilled and fiercely strong). Eventually we all stumbled back, tumbled into bed and fell asleep.

Diana, who was lying in the darkness on one side of the bed, with the mosquito net for company, suddenly felt alert. She was sure that I (who was in the middle of the bed) had subtly shifted closer to her. Was it true? She was slightly paranoid from the weed, and Kev and I both seemed to be fast asleep, but she was sure that I seemed a bit closer.

She lay there in the darkness, staring up at the mosquito net. She shifted to try and make herself comfortable – and there it was again. Stuart was closer! Definitely! What could she do? She was so stupid – stuck in a foreign country, having voluntarily got into bed with a guy she obviously didn't know that well. But still, surely he wasn't going to try anything? Not with his mate in the same *bed*? By now, she was holding her breath. She tried to move subtly away but found that I was by now practically next to her and breathing down her neck.

Finally at the point of desperation, she felt me move again and thought, this is it, here it comes, there's nothing I can do. At that moment I said huskily into her ear: "Diana, can you get off my pillow?"

She got up on her elbow and saw that in her stoned state

she had fidgeted almost all the way into the middle of the bed, shovelling all three of us into an uncomfortably tight squish with each other. She moved back to her side of the bed, buried her head under her pillow in embarrassment and was not disturbed by my attentions again.

My best friend went on a skiing holiday back in his early 20s. He'd been skiing before but not in France, and was caught unawares by the type of French toilet that predominated at the resort. One morning when the whole group was getting ready before setting out for the slopes, he went to the toilet and was horrified to find that, after he had flushed, there was a really quite sizeable "movement" that refused to budge. He waited and flushed again to no avail, until people started knocking on the loo door to tell him to hurry up.

Not sure what to do, he pretended he was feeling a bit ill and sent the others on ahead, saying he'd catch them up. What he couldn't get his head round was that in the loo there was a sort of shelf, which seemed made deliberately to stop anything getting flushed away.

He waited for the cistern to fill up again, and flushed. And waited again, and flushed. He kept doing this until he'd been on his own for almost half an hour and was starting to get a bit desperate, now thinking that he was doing something wrong, but what he had left there was so monstrously large that he couldn't contemplate leaving without having dealt with it. At last the French maid appeared to clean up the chalet and after prevaricating for a few more minutes from inside the toilet he opened the door and, speaking no French at all, beckoned to her to come over. He pointed at what was in the loo, made a wild uncomprehending gesture to express his state of bafflement and then flushed the toilet. It disappeared at once and as the maid looked up at him rather confused, he realised that it looked as though he had been waiting to show off its size to someone, before flushing it away. Unable to say anything to put her right about this, he had to slink out of the chalet as she began tidying up, casting him strange looks as he went.

C.R.

Last year I was on a night bus home when a very large man asked if he could sit down next to me. I smiled politely and then turned to look out the window. He tapped me on the shoulder, introduced himself as Lips and asked if he could show me a picture of his house. Not wanting to offend, I nodded, and he pulled out a photo of the White House.

Realising that he was clearly insane, I smiled and nodded and turned back to the window. Then he started asking me if I spoke Spanish. I said no, so as not to prolong the conversation, so then he told me to start repeating simple phrases after him. Well aware that the rest of the bus was listening to our conversation, I was speaking extra quietly, only for him to keep saying "Speak up! I can't hear you! Say it again!" so I ended up basically shouting random Spanish phrases to the rest of the bus. When we finally got near my stop, I got up to leave but he wouldn't let me past until I agreed to give him my phone number so he could call me to continue our Spanish "lessons".

Thinking on my feet, I gave him a false number and could only stare at him awkwardly as he rang the number on loudspeaker and everyone on the bus listened to the electronic voice say, "This number has not been recognised. Please try again." I then had to feign stupidity – "Oh I must have given you my old one! Silly me" – before giving him my real number. He rang me about 60 times that weekend. Worried that he knew where I lived, having seen me get off the bus, and

> that he might hunt me down and kill me, I eventually
> made my housemate answer the phone and tell him
> some elaborate story that culminated in me having
> moved to Bristol, leaving my phone behind.
> **E.M.**

*   *   *

Transport is a massive issue for the person susceptible to awkward situations. It brings you into close contact with thousands of people from every walk of life. And if you're the type of person to whom these things always happen, they'll definitely happen on a train or bus sooner or later. As the following, rather intensely horrible, middle class nightmare proves.

This happened late last summer. I was on a packed bus on my way to Liverpool Street station in London for a weekend away and a woman got on the bus who, with the evidence at my disposal, is very hard not to describe as a drug-addled prostitute.

The bus had only gone about 200 yards when she decided to get off, so she started shouting to the driver to open the door between stops. This was on the back of the 149, which is a bendy bus, and it was packed. The driver was miles away and couldn't hear her. She then pulled the cover off the emergency stop button instead but the people all around her started shouting so she lost interest in that and came to stand opposite me. The bus travelled on in peace for about ten seconds before she got bored.

"Officer! Officer!" she said to me. "You an officer?"

"No," I said, and carried on playing a game on my iPhone called Mini-Gore (it's from the genre of games called "zombie mayhem"; its tagline is *Thousands of Them ... One of You*).

"Officer! Officer!" she said again. "Officer!"

I carried on playing.

"Officer, can you get him to let me off? Can you get him to let me off here, officer, please?" She had a voice that was loud and whiney but slightly blurred at the same time. I decided I couldn't look up from the game or I'd be trapped in a conversation I couldn't control.

After a short pause she went on. "Do you know me, officer? Do you recognise me? Am I better looking than my form sheet?" Pause. "Am I a bit older? Won't you look at me, officer?"

To add effect she drew the word out in a wheedling East End accent, getting longer each time she said it. Offissah. Offissaah. Offissaaargh.

I should point out:

1. I was on my way for a weekend with family friends with just my rucksack, and was wearing an extra jumper and coat that I couldn't fit into my bag.

2. I was extremely late, as I'd reached the bus stop earlier only to discover that my phone had run out of

battery. I'd gone back, couldn't find my charger, spent an hour looking in shops for a replacement and had then had to wait a further 40 minutes for my phone to charge up again, and I was severely stressed into the bargain.

3. It was a hot August Saturday afternoon and the bus (as I've mentioned) was packed from front to back.

4. Thanks to the awkwardness of the situation, I was concentrating so furiously on my game that I was rapidly approaching my highest-ever score.

The combination of all these factors meant I was sweating very profusely. Droplets were dangling unattended at the end of my nose like a marathon runner who's too tired to swipe them away.

Seeing this, the woman changed gear. She spoke more quietly. "You sweatin', officer?" she asked. She took a step forward. "Are you sweatin'?" she repeated. She came forward until her face was right next to mine, unnaturally close. "Am I making you sweat?" she asked. More and more zombies came upon the scene and with ruthless efficiency I massacred them all, carving a line of safety through each approaching horde.

"I'll make you sweat," said the woman, as I sweated still harder, and she began to dance around me, a bit like a pole dance but without actually touching me. "You sweating now?" she said. I killed zombie after zombie after zombie.

By now there was nowhere further for this to go. She was so close to me, and had done so much to get my attention, that the only things left for her to do were to head butt me or walk away. The bus shuddered to a halt and her mate, who had been watching with amusement all along, said, "Come on." And they got off.

I carried on playing the game rather than risk meeting anyone else's eyes on the still-heaving bus, and began to feel a growing euphoria. I had been in the middle of a social nightmare and without actually doing anything I'd totally won. I hadn't lost my dignity or been humiliated – in fact, the shackles of self-consciousness and hesitancy had brilliantly made me seem like an imperturbable man of steel, not the awkward creep I really was! Hahah! And what's more I had completely *smashed* my best ever score on Mini-Gore.

*   *   *

I was on one of those middle class gap years after uni, where you visit countless fascinating countries with a huge amount to offer and yet somehow only manage to take in the beaches and drinking spots. I enjoyed myself but was still quite young and reserved – unlike my mate Finn. Wherever we were he regularly got wasted and ended up coming back to the hostel we were staying in much later than us and in a truly terrible state.

The first night we stayed in Singapore was no exception. Convinced he remembered where his bunk was in the dark, he dived into it. Unfortunately for him there was a guy already in the bed, who kicked him out onto the floor. Too drunk and exhausted to get up again, Finn fell asleep. Roused by the voices of other people in the dorm getting up to go sightseeing, he woke up seven hours later with the whole place lit up by sunshine to find that he was lying in the space between beds, completely naked with a hard-on.

As his travelling companions we thought this was funny enough, but he couldn't live it down because of something that had happened once before, in student halls: in the first week at uni, he'd come back completely pissed one night and picked the wrong door on the corridor. Then he'd taken off his clothes and got into bed with the guy (who had already passed out, totally drunk) whose room it actually was. They'd woken up with their arms around each other and neither of them with any memory of how they had ended up that way.

C.P.

My dad used to drive me to school because he worked quite nearby. This arrangement worked all through primary school but a week or so after I started at secondary school, which was on the opposite side of the road, he was away on business and my mum had to take me. This added a lot to her day and made her quite stressed as she drove through the school-run traffic to drop me right up at the gates. I got out and went to make my way into the playground past the entire year group from the year above me, who were gathered there for some kind of day trip. I was already on the school steps, about 20 yards away, when I heard my mum's voice. I looked back to see her leaning out of the window, feeling guilty that she had been so distracted in the car and calling out: "Darling, I'm sorry we haven't had any Mummy schnoo-time!"

With that she drove off. The whole of the year above stared at me. My future career at that school was set from that moment on.

N.F.

I was on the train back from my parents' house in Essex after Christmas, happily listening to my iPod, when a woman wearing a tracksuit, with big gold rings, greasy hair and HATE tattooed on her knuckles, sat down opposite me and started talking to me, asking me where I was heading. I explained that I was going back to London, and she nodded and launched into a monologue about how Christmas was really hard for her because her husband had died this time last year and that, now her child was in care, she hardly saw him anymore.

I started to say I was sorry to hear that but she continued straight on, saying, "And then two of my brothers were killed in Afghanistan last year. When they told me, I stormed straight to Heathrow and tried to get a flight out there. I had to be restrained by three policemen." Feeling really quite awkward now, and aware that the rest of the train could hear everything I was saying, I told her I was sorry again and that it sounded terrible.

Again she carried on talking, telling me that we were going past the place where her father was buried — at which point she stopped talking, waved out the window and said "Rest in peace, Dad," before asking me to join her in prayer for him. I was sweating profusely with the pure discomfort of the whole situation but, not wanting to offend lest she punched me, I did as she asked.

By now I was certain that the situation couldn't get any worse, but it did – she started crying. Not quite sure what I should do or say, and knowing full well I couldn't move seats as I'd already said I was travelling to London and I could hardly leave a crying woman, I sat there in awkward silence for the remainder of the journey while she sobbed opposite me.

L.H.

My housemates and I were going to a party and because as per usual we were running late and it was raining, we decided to get a cab instead of the tube. We were a little bit drunk and in high spirits, so chatted loudly to the cab driver during the journey. When we got to the party, he asked us what time we'd be leaving as he'd come and pick us up. Knowing what a nightmare it is to get cabs in London on a Saturday night, my housemates and I agreed enthusiastically (perhaps overly so) and named a time of three a.m.

At about two a.m. we decided to leave and head to McDonalds. After we'd attractively chomped through our food, we saw an empty cab so decided to take that one instead of waiting 20 minutes for the one we'd originally booked. When three a.m. came round our original cab driver started calling Kiren to say he was there and waiting for us; Kiren told him that we were sorry, but we'd already left. She hung up. He rang again. She didn't pick up. He rang another eight times.

We dismissed it as a slightly weird but funny tale and the next weekend we all went to a friend's BBQ. Again running late, we ordered a cab. About five minutes into our journey, the cab driver suddenly said, "You girls don't remember who I am, do you?" And we suddenly clicked that yes, it was the same cab driver as before — and boy, was he angry. He ranted at us for about ten minutes about how cruel and selfish we were, how he'd lost money waiting for us that night and now, when anyone asked him what was the worst moment of his job, he would identify that one occasion.

As the token spokesperson I apologised profusely, to which he replied, "I don't want your apologies. Stop. I don't want to hear it. All I want is for you heartless, selfish girls to give a little money to charity."

"We will," I replied. And then there didn't seem to be anything left to say, so we all sat there in awkward silence for the rest of the journey, until we got to our friend's house and tipped him 20 quid in our hurry to get out.

C.S.

My friend Matt was in a carpark the other day and went to leave. When he got to the barrier he realised he was slightly too far away to reach to put his ticket in the machine. Unfortunately, as he was straining out the window, a gust of wind blew the ticket out of his outstretched fingers. Matt had no choice but to get out of the car, blocking the only exit, and spend the next twenty minutes chasing the ticket round the carpark, in full view of the queue of enraged drivers that had built up behind his car, honking their horns and occasionally swearing, which panicked Matt so much that when he finally got back into the car, he was so stressed out that he stalled about eight times and it took him a further ten minutes to get the car moving again.

H.B.

MISCELLANEOUS NIGHTMARES

SPORT

In my attempts to unearth other people's embarrassing stories, I've discovered that it seems other people don't really humiliate themselves in sporting endeavours as much as I do.

Coming from a very sporting family (where everyone else, including my mum, is not only better at sport than me but actually genuinely very good at sport), my humiliations in this field began young, if only because my family first assumed that being related to them I must be talented at some kind of sport. When this proved not to be the case they thought I would turn out to be good at it, and must be encouraged to persevere. It took the duration of my whole childhood to prove them wrong.

My first and only sporting medal is for being the runner up at a putting competition when I was four years old. The winner (probably being naturally talented) managed to get a hole from a teeing-off point at the edge of the green in six or seven strokes, and I seem to remember that all of the other children had dropped out (or run away) in varying levels of tearfulness, meaning that I was runner-up by default. It only remained for me to finish the competition, which in the under-fives category meant getting the ball in the hole, just once.

It was August in the west of Ireland and therefore raining and ice-cold on the golf course, so when my dad put his hands over mine on the putter and showed me how to hit the ball without smacking it 30 feet off the green, no-one protested. I eventually got the hole in 32 shots.

In my personal history of sporting embarrassment, however, the main action is concentrated on the cricket field. In my mid-teens I had a brief spell of enthusiasm for cricket, partly because the standard of our local club's Sunday 2nds team was encouragingly low and there prevailed a mood of happy and none-too-competitive amateurism. No-one expected you to be that good and, indeed, quite often you could be cheerfully congratulated for being crap. Into this forgiving atmosphere I brought an idiosyncratic style and ineptitude that managed to try even their considerable patience.

I started well, though. Out of nowhere in my first or

second game I turned in a good performance and took three wickets (for something like 20 runs – which if you don't know cricket is pretty good, by the way, for a beginner) bowling leg spin. This didn't ingratiate me however, because at the time I was playing for the other side. They had turned up several men short, discovered me reading a P.G. Wodehouse novel on the boundary, invited me to make up their numbers and given me a bowl out of courtesy.

I was always actually rather proud of my bowling because, although I wasn't often asked to bring it out, it almost always got wickets. This was due to my looping style of delivery, which was so unthreatening it somehow made time stand still. When the ball left my hand the batsman would realise this was what he'd been waiting for – the one you could hit for six. "Actually," he would think, "this one's coming so slow, I can choose where I clear the boundary, where's best or most impressive to get the six, or where's the least defended." And then he would make his choice, get into position and raise the bat. And the ball still wouldn't be with him. At last he would get jittery, his mind wildly over-thinking the shot and he would scoop it high into the air for a catch, or miss it entirely and get stumped.

The better the batsman, the worse it undid them because they couldn't help over-thinking it. It was very satisfying – except that on that particular day it was my own "team mates" I was getting out. It didn't help that my performance made the local paper too, where I was nominated a "schoolboy spinner".

By the time I actually got to play on the right side, I was no longer suffering any glitches of good form and sank back into my former state of humble ineptitude. While fielding in one of my first games, the ball was hit past me and towards the boundary. As I sprinted after it I experienced that little thrill that you occasionally get as a fielder, when you see that the ball is beginning to slow enough for you to reach it just before it gets to the boundary. What's especially exciting about this is that you get to dive or slide and flick it back behind you, sometimes with mere centimetres to spare. Just like a goalkeeper tipping the ball around a post, you get to be heroic, physically... graceful, stylish and cool.

Readying myself as I came within a few feet of the ball, with the rope only a couple of yards beyond it, I angled my body and leapt forward knee-first to slide stylishly alongside the ball and turn it back. I was so certain that this was going to be a textbook finish that I remember I was feeling a bit smug as my knee slid against the ground and bounced into an invisible hummock. I think I even let out a kind of startled "hurp!" noise like a cartoon character as my knee caught and sent me spinning over, collecting the ball as I went and taking us both over the boundary for four runs. The other players enjoyed watching it so much they gave me the "Moment of the Match" award, for which I received a half-bottle of Sainsbury's cava. I could tell this was the right team for me.

In the following game I was caught out in a slightly worse way. I was fielding again, this time at the boundary on the leg side, and the batsman cut the ball hard in the opposite direction. Hundreds of yards away on the other side of the pitch, fielders started to scurry around. That meant I was safe so I retreated ten feet or so to one of the white wooden blocks that are spaced every ten yards around the boundary. From behind it I retrieved my pint of bitter and a smouldering cigarette and took a sip and a relaxing lungful of smoke, at which point I heard people shouting from the centre of the pitch and noticed the ball gently trundling past me over the boundary, a few feet away. The fielder on the other side had massively over-thrown and, following the ball, everyone's eyes had fallen on me staring away in the other direction with drink and cigarette in hand, looking slightly startled to be caught out and generally more like someone who's come to a party dressed as a cricketer than someone who was actually in the middle of a game.

Those were beginner's efforts, though. My sporting career didn't have long to go but it was to reach a kind of apotheosis a few months later. I have 4 brothers; 11 years separate eldest and youngest and I'm number 4 of 5. My younger brother was just coming into the local team at this point, my dad had recently played a few games for the first time in 20 years and enjoyed them more than he had expected, and my eldest brother was back in the country after teaching abroad for several years and eager to play. All of a sudden it seemed there was a chance all six members of the same family might turn out on the same day for the same team. We mentioned this to the local club and quicker than we expected they were able to accommodate us.

It was the kind of day made for cricket, a calm bright midsummer Sunday, hot in the sun and cool in the shade. The ground was dotted with oaks, under which deck chairs were stretched, and a happy post-tea languor prevailed among the spectators. My brother Greg had brought his new Australian girlfriend to meet the family for the first time in this most English of settings; she sat watching us next to my mum. And it was Greg himself who was coming in to bowl when, fielding at mid-on, I felt a sharp sting on my right buttock.

I managed to stay still and watched him bowl, trying to work out why the hell my trousers were stinging me. It wasn't that hard to work out: there was a wasp up there. The batsman blocked the ball, and it was thrown back to the bowler. I took this punctuation to slap my own behind as hard as I could, easily hard enough to crush an insect caught there. No-one as far as I could tell had noticed me hitting myself on the arse – or maybe they thought it was some kind of applause.

Greg walked back to bowl the next ball and like all the other fielders I took ten steps backwards to regain my original position, but shaking my leg all the way to try and get rid of the wasp carcass, thinking to myself something like: this is the sort of thing that always bloody happens to me but this time I've spared myself by remaining cool. So fuck you, fate!

As Greg came in to bowl the next ball and I took four or five steps toward the batsman, I felt another sharp sting on my buttock. I could put up with the pain and try slapping myself repeatedly, but this could end up going on all afternoon. So it was quite an easy decision to jump on the ground, drag my trousers off, and wave them around until the wasp was gone. Although it may have detracted somewhat from my family's special occasion, it definitely augmented the afternoon's experience for everyone else who was there.

NEIGHBOURS

I've been living in my flat for nearly a year now. Being a disorganised sort of person, it's only now I've pretty much finally unpacked and settled in. But I'm stuck in a difficult situation, in which I'm trapped by my own middle class upbringing.

Last summer (when I'd been here four months or so) someone from the flat above started spitting down onto my third-floor bedroom window. It was hot and the window was open more or less all the time so the spit landed and dried on, leaving a conspicuous stain. I thought this was pretty rude and annoying, but felt it could just about have been accidental – or rather the unintentional result of spitting out of the window.

Then came shaving foam – a languorous loop of it sprayed down onto my window from above with a roll-up cigarette dropped in the top, like a garnish. Rain refused to come and over a few days the heavy heat fused the foam into a sticky grey glue, with the cigarette (which, now I think about it, looked more like a joint) stuck at eye level. The window is hinged at the top so it's very hard to reach around it to clean the outside, although I thought I might possibly be able to reach it from my balcony with a mop. But that thought gave rise to another problem: what good would cleaning it do? It would simply give my upstairs neighbour a fresh canvas to work with. He was already adding to his current effort with further instances of energetic spitting.

I was now in a proper middle class conundrum. Totally unused to confrontation or having to protect my territory, I had no idea how to go about bringing up the matter with the people upstairs. I had never met any of them, or even seen them, before. I could be rising to the bait and giving them an excuse to break down my door and kill me (it didn't help that at the time I was reading a book about Katrina Marino, the New York woman who lived in a block of flats like mine and was murdered in the courtyard watched by over a dozen witnesses, none of whom called the police).

Either way I thought that generally my upstairs neighbour was waiting for a reaction. Maybe so they could escalate the conflict. Shaving foam and spitting I could handle, but what if it then got worse? It also seemed a shame for my first contact with any of my neighbours to be a complaint about them.

While I was worrying about what I would do if it got worse, it got a bit worse. Enough for me to take photos, but not to show them to anyone. They poured down what looked like a pot of strawberry yoghurt drink, which was mostly washed off a few days later. Then came what looked like big handfuls of paper towel, soaked and thrown hard so they exploded on the window.

I fantasised about staying awake all night (which the heat often made happen anyway) in order to catch and photograph him doing it. I imagined catching him when he leant out of the window and hitting him really hard with a tennis ball. A tennis ball is somehow the perfect weapon to throw really hard at someone, as it leaves no lasting damage, genuinely hurts, and looks funny when it bounces off their head. (It's not lost on me that my revenge delivery system was itself definingly middle class. In my uglier moments I dreamt of throwing a cricket ball in its place.)

But I knew I wouldn't have the guts to do it. Chances are it would turn out to be a 13-year-old boy and I'd blind him, or he'd fall out of the window and I'd be charged with manslaughter. Or I'd somehow end up being sued or in prison. Invariably, I felt, such nervous middle class types manage to screw everything up and end up the worse for it.

Eventually, my flatmate and I decided to have a belated house-warming and I made up my mind that this was the moment to go upstairs and make contact. Henry and I discussed it for a while. Equally middle class, he suggested that I should invite them to come along. I thought that was taking insincerity and politeness too far.

I went up the flight of stairs and knocked on the door. There was no answer. Behind the clouded glass I could see figures moving back and forth. After a couple of minutes, not quite sure what to do, I knocked again. Once more I could see figures going to and fro behind the glass, ignoring the door.

Finally the door cracked. It went back about ten centimetres on the chain, but no face appeared. Whoever it was didn't say anything.

"Hello?" I said.

"Hello," said a voice. From the voice and the shape I could roughly see through the window, it looked like a teenage boy. Beside him was what looked like another boy.

"Hi, I'm from the flat downstairs, I just wanted to let

you know we're going to have a party tonight that might go on quite late, so sorry for the noise."

"Right," he said.

Seizing my chance, I added, "And can you tell whoever it is to stop dropping stuff on my window."

"I don't know anything about that," he said.

"Yes you do. It's coming from the bedroom right behind you so whoever is in there is doing it, can you ask them to stop, thanks."

"Uright," he said, and closed the door. I could hear laughter behind it as I retreated down the stairs.

The party didn't go on that late and wouldn't have disturbed anyone. My parents were there for much of the evening, and there wasn't a single breakage or spillage.

The weather broke soon after and the boy from upstairs (I now realised it was him I was dealing with) never got back into the swing of dropping stuff on my windows. I did eventually see his dad, who was every bit as terrifying as I had feared – as muscly, tattoed and bejewelled as the sitcom stereotype of a thug.

As I write this the window is above me, still uncleaned and looking disgustingly pocked and smeared with sun-dried effluvia. Aside from having to explain it to a few girlfriends and sensing that my masculinity was somewhat diminished by the tale, I don't really mind. I tend to keep the curtains closed. I'll probably wash it off with a long-handled mop in the summer and wait to see what happens next. The chances are it'll start up again immediately afterwards, and I still won't do anything.

*   *   *

I share my street front door with a neighbour who lives in the flat above me. My doorbell was out of action for a while so sometimes visitors rang his when I didn't answer. One day last summer my neighbour answered it in his towel and alas, the door to his flat slammed shut behind him, locking him out. I found him in the shared corridor after some frantic knocking at my flat door. The poor guy was mortified.

The girl he'd let in for me was a prospective flatmate coming to look at my spare room, and her face was an absolute picture as they both came into my flat together. He was stuck just in his little towel and he asked if I had any clothes he could borrow so he could try and climb onto his roof terrace from my balcony. Bearing in mind I'm five foot two while he is six foot four and built like a brick shithouse, you can imagine how funny he looked in a tiny t-shirt that showed his midriff and tracksuit bottoms that came to just below his knees. For a big, macho guy he couldn't have looked more gay if he'd tried, which just made the whole thing even more mortifying for him.

After a lot of trying we couldn't manage to climb onto the balcony so he had to sit in my living room in his funny little outfit while I "interviewed" the prospective flatmate over a polite cup of tea. He called his sister and she eventually came to his rescue with a spare key, but he was so embarrassed and no matter how much I tried to comfort him and tell him it didn't matter, he couldn't see the funny side of it at all.

The prospective flatmate loved the flat and moved in a couple of weeks later. The neighbour moved out a couple of weeks after that.

H.C.

SCHOOL

Once when we were very young and at primary school, my friends and I played this really horrible trick on our mate Chris. It was a school assembly and the head teacher was talking but Chris wasn't paying attention to what was being said and was instead muttering to the kid next to him. Suddenly, a friend on the other side of him tapped his shoulder and whispered, "Hey Chris, they've called your name – you've won a prize!"

Chris, naturally happy to learn this, stood up and shuffled his way along the row, then walked up the side of the hall to the front while 200 slightly puzzled children watched him. He reached the front and when the head teacher asked him what he was doing he confidently told him that he was there to collect his prize. The head teacher just stared at him.

Realising something was not right, he turned round and looked across to the back of the room where we sat, convulsed with laughter and waving. He then began the slow, humiliating walk back to his seat, in front of the whole school.

S.P.

Susie Stupples was an incredibly gorgeous girl who was in the same year as me at school. I'd adored her from afar for years and when I was 14, she sat next to me in Biology GCSE class. Having longed to be near her and have the chance to talk, I was overcome with nerves and spent the whole course utterly refusing to meet her gaze, let alone speak to her.

When the two years were nearly at an end, she came into school one day wearing a new blue sweater that made her eyes shine even more beautifully than before. I knew I didn't have much time left so, stealing myself with superhuman resolve, I forced myself to say, "That's a nice jumper!"

It came out more like a shout than a casual remark and she turned her beautiful eyes to me and said, "It's nice isn't it? Angora." She held her arm up to me. "Feel it," she offered. I was a horrible parody of gawky adolescence at the time – face like a battlefield of acne, huge ugly bouffant of ginger hair, voice squeaking like a badly played violin, and I was quivering with nerves into the bargain. So instead of gently rubbing the material between forefinger and thumb, I grabbed her forearm and gripped it. She looked at me, startled.

"What are you doing?" she said. But I was so nervous I couldn't let go, and she started to get a bit scared. I stared at her arm and carried on gripping it for a while longer, until I could force my hand to release. Then I turned away, unable to offer any explanation, and avoided her eye for the rest of the time we shared a desk.

T.W.

My parents sent me to a comprehensive school near where I lived because it was Catholic and so were they, but they were quite well off and had (still have in fact) what is by most people's standards quite an enormous house in a very leafy, tucked-away part of the suburbs. I hated this ostentatious sign of how much better off we were than my classmates, and for years avoided having people round if I could help it. When my friends' parents drove me home I would always ask to be dropped at the end of the road so that they wouldn't catch sight of the house. That is, until one day when I wasn't paying attention and the next thing I knew we were pulling up outside.

"Wow, Diana!" said my friend's dad. "Is that your place? It's lovely!"

"No," I said, panicking, "that's the main house. Some rich family live there. We live in that little building alongside."

"Oh," said my friend's mum, obviously feeling bad that they'd been so insensitive. "Well, it's nice to see you, hopefully see you again soon!"

I thanked her, got out of the car and ran towards the house. But of course they stayed to watch me all the way to the door to make sure someone was in. So I had to go to the building attached to the side of our house, which was actually large enough for a family to live in, and let myself in. It was our garage. I waited inside until the car had driven off and then went shame-facedly back to the house.

D.P.

My family aren't known for our acting talent, and my elder brother Tom arguably least of all. Unfortunately for us, it was our school's policy that every child had to take part in the school play in some way, and for some inexplicable reason, when the Head of Drama decided to put on Charlie and the Chocolate Factory one year, he cast Tom as an Oompa Loompa.

Months of rehearsals followed, where Tom desperately tried to get to grips with the singing, dancing and general co-ordination that the part required. The opening night finally came and my parents, realising that this was an opportunity that they probably wouldn't get again, had front row seats. On came Tom, painted orange and dressed in a garish outfit complete with striped pop socks. As vaguely anticipated, he was slightly out of time with the dance moves, and didn't seem entirely

confident of the words, but wasn't doing too badly —
until midway through one song, when he sidestepped
too far to the left, fell off the stage into the orchestra pit,
destroying a variety of instruments and bringing the
entire production to a standstill. My parents left at
the interval.

E.M.

OUT AND ABOUT

One day in the school holidays, during my horrible,
horrible adolescence, I went out for a walk near our
house on the south coast. Like a lot of boys, for me
this whole period was one of unremitting self-loathing,
awkwardness and hatred of the world in general. But
that day it was the beginning of the holidays, I had
INXS on cassette in my walkman — to my mind, the
cutting edge of musical cool — and during that walk all
of a sudden everything seemed wondrously okay. The
sun was shining, there was a soft breeze and wildlife
stirred in every direction. I was overcome by a
moment of euphoria — it was good to be alive! I
started to run, propelled by joy. As I ran I saw a stick

by the side of the path up ahead and I decided I was going to kick it, just out of sheer happiness.

As I reached the stick, I swung my leg with full force – and missed. And it wasn't a stick, it was a rusty iron bar that was sticking out of a concrete block that had been left there. It connected with the centre of my shin and sent me catapulting over onto my back, writhing and frothing in agony, with INXS still blaring in my ears, feeling like a judgement had been passed down upon me for letting go for an instant, and trying to be happy.
T.W.

My friend Sarah was shopping in Selfridges one day after work when she suddenly realised she couldn't find her bag. It was one of those cotton totes – the type that women often use in addition to their normal handbags – with blue and white checks, and it contained various things that she was bringing back from the office. She panicked, because there was a lot of important paperwork inside, and started retracing her steps through the store, trying to work out if she'd left it anywhere. She ran back through her whole route

but couldn't spot it. Eventually, in desperation, she approached the nearest sales desk and asked the (rather superior-looking) assistant if anyone had handed in a blue and white chequered bag. "What, like that one?" said the sales assistant, pointing to Sarah's shoulder. She looked down, and realised that the bag had been over her arm the entire time. Wishing the ground would open and swallow her whole, she took a deep breath, thanked the girl and made a swift exit.
O.B.

PETS

I really want to come clean about this – I'm not going to actually *tell* my brother and sister-in-law but I'm writing it down so there's a chance they will read it and know my shame. It's time the truth was told.

About two years ago my brother Tom asked me to look after his and his girlfriend's flat and to cat-sit for a few weeks over the Christmas holidays. I said that would be fine, but I was already looking after our other brother's cat for the first day and a half that he wanted me there.

"That's fine," he said, "if you get there on the Saturday, it'll be fine."

"You mean the cat will be okay just running around outside for a few days?"

"Nnnno," he said. "Actually there's a cat next door that likes to terrorise our one. So we keep the cat-flap shut up in case he gets in. But it'll be fine, I promise."

I took him at his word, although I was a bit dubious, and planned to get there on Saturday morning when I had been relieved of my duty at Greg's house.

Now, this took place in the weird twilight zone that is the week between Christmas and New Year, when you forget what day it is, and it starts to feel like a strange endless holiday, especially if you're staying in a London with nobody in it. On the Friday night, as is my habit, I went out with my friends who had stayed in the city. For some reason, probably because we'd all been cooped up in our homes for a few days, it became a big night, went on till about four in the morning and we all got really smashed. I kept telling people how weird it was that I was supposed to be house-sitting a cat that had been trapped inside on its own for 24 hours and how guilty I felt about it.

When I woke up at two in the afternoon the next day, I didn't feel like going anywhere. The brother who I was currently house-sitting for came home and relieved me of my duty, but I couldn't bear the thought of dragging my bones through the freezing weather to my other brother's house. As the day wore on I felt progressively worse. I considered that the cat couldn't possibly be feeling as bad as me, so told myself not to feel guilty about it.

By eight p.m. I was a bit better, and my phone rang. It was a friend telling me that we were supposed to be going out tonight. I'd totally forgotten until he said so – but yes, now I thought about it, indeed we were. I'd planned to be ensconced in Tom's house by now and ready to go out. What's more, now I was feeling okay for the first time today, I felt I owed it to myself to have a good time. As I caught the bus towards the pub I think my reasoning was that the cat had been on its own in the flat for so long by now, that a little bit longer wasn't going to make a difference. I stayed out all night.

The next day I approached Tom's flat with extreme trepidation, worrying that I would find the animal starved to death, possibly with its claws stuck to the inside of the door. When I got in, there it was. Alive. A bit surly, and unhappy, but that seemed to be the extent of the cat's reprisals. Until I found that it had shat on my brother's bed. Ever the coward, I decided that as I was sleeping in the spare room, and turd removal was not within the remit of my unpaid position, I left it there for three weeks and then pretended afterwards that I'd never noticed it.

I felt so bad about the cat, however, and was so anxious to make it feel better, that I fed it a tin of tuna every day for the rest of my stay. Apparently you're not supposed to that; it's far too much food. In the course of those three weeks it became, in my sister-in-law's words, "noticeably fat," and remains to this day dangerously overweight.

About six years ago some friends of mine asked me to house-sit for them while they went on a long holiday to Vietnam. I had just finished studying and had nowhere to live at the time so it was perfect for me. The three weeks were almost like heaven and luckily I got on wonderfully with the pet dog in my charge – until the inevitable catastrophe.

About five days before they were due back, the dog began looking really unwell. He kept being sick everywhere, so I took him to the vet. After the vet had checked him over, he came out to give me the bad news: the animal was very, very sick, and there was nothing he could do – it was going to die.

I had to take the dog home with me and try and look after it that night, knowing I'd only have to bring it in again tomorrow to be put down. I was really upset, though at the same time I could see I was in a classic sitcom-style predicament and that if it were a comedy, I'd be trying to replace the dog and getting myself into a Basil Fawlty-type farcical situation. I knew what I had to do and so, in between bouts of crying, I phoned my friends in Vietnam and broke the news to them. They were devastated but they understood it wasn't my fault.

I asked them what I should do with the dog's remains – I had assumed (as had the vet) that I would leave the body at the surgery to be disposed of, but the owners were distraught at the idea. They wanted to bury him in the back garden and begged me to bring the dog back home. I said yes, of course, and wondered to myself how I was going to manage this without a car.

The next day I had the grim task of taking the dog along to the vet along with a bag that was big enough to carry him home in (which I tested by surreptitiously measuring him against it). When it was done, I was given the body and had to cram it into my enormous rucksack. He only just fitted; I had to squeeze his head in, and when I picked it up the bag was agonisingly heavy.

I caught a cab to the tube and just about managed to get the bag on the train but when I got off at the other end, there was a flight of stairs out of the station. I must have looked like I was struggling because this guy came up and offered to help me with it. I was incredibly grateful and as we went up the stairs we chatted.

"God, it's heavy," he said, "what have you got in here?"

"Oh," I said, thinking rapidly, "I'm between flats and staying at a friend's for a week. Just stuff – clothes, shoes, books, my laptop..."

The second I mentioned the word "laptop" he was

off, sprinting up the steps and out into the street with
the bag on his back.
H.F.

CHARITY

I was coming out of a pub late one night, in a state
where my sympathies were easily aroused, and as
I walked I realised the woman walking near me
was crying inconsolably. She was very pale, in her
early 30s and wearing a white tracksuit. After we had
been walking 100 yards or so and she was still crying
– properly bawling her eyes out – it became
ridiculous for me not to say something, so I asked her
if she was alright.

"No," she said, still crying miserably, "I've just got
out of prison and found out I've got breast cancer and
my boyfriend's kicked me out. I haven't got a penny
and I just need two quid to get a bus to my mum's,
south of the river." This sequence of events was so
viciously unfair that I was kind of winded by it and
gave her the money without thinking about it. She
thanked me for it. I said no worries, and I hoped
everything would be okay.

We were still both walking in the same direction so
we continued in silence (except for her crying and

sniffing) for about two minutes longer. It was now about two a.m. and the only shop open on the street was the late night off-licence. As we reached it she swerved right in front of me and went straight in, without saying a word.

* * *

When I was at university, one night I nipped out of the student union nightclub onto the main street to get some cash. While I was in the queue I got talking to a worryingly youthful boy who was sleeping rough. He seemed completely normal and nice, just very unhappy – he'd run away from a violent stepfather. The unfairness of it was utterly plain to me and the fact that we had a bedroom in our student house not being slept in seemed a monstrous inequality. I promised to take him home with us when we left the club and instructed him where to meet me. Then I went back in and explained it to my housemates.

They stared at me like I was an idiot. "He's not coming back with us," one of them said.

"But he's fine! Seriously, he's a nice lad, he's just having a horrible time. We're just giving him a roof for one night."

"He'll nick stuff," said another with ruthless finality. This seemed completely unfair to my new friend. Then I thought about it, and felt moral compromise stealing over me like a grey cloud. I knew that if I was in the homeless guy's position, I would be tempted to steal something, and that actually there was no way we could risk inviting him into the house. I said I should go out and tell him the bad news.

"Don't mate," they said. "He'll just try and persuade you again." I didn't think this was true – I had offered the place to stay without him asking after all, but I knew if I went back out and tried to explain it, I wouldn't be able to and would come back in doubly persuaded that he should stay. And then be persuaded back the other way again by the boys once I came back in. So I didn't go. We stayed for a few more drinks, then snuck out the other exit.

When we were about seventeen my mate Jaxx and I decided to hold a dinner party for about ten of our friends. We decided to keep things simple and cook spaghetti bolognaise, but thought we'd make the most amazing sauce completely from scratch. We started cooking at about 4pm, and slowly worked our way through the red wine that we'd been intending to put in the sauce. Hours later, we had the most perfect bolognaise sauce – but by this time being quite drunk, we managed to completely over-cook the pasta. The resulting white sticky mess was absolutely disgusting, and our friends valiantly pushed it around their plates until eventually everyone conceded defeat. By this time, much more red wine had been consumed, and Jaxx and I decided that now was the perfect time to commit an act of charity, and donate the unwanted spag bol to the tramp who regularly camped outside the flat. We put it in a plastic bowl and approached the tramp. 'Excuse me,' I said, 'would you like some spaghetti bolognaise? We've made you some.' In hindsight it's clear just how ridiculous this situation was, but at the time we genuinely thought we were being friendly and helpful. The tramp took the bowl somewhat doubtfully, sniffed it and said, 'It's cold. Why the fuck are you trying to give me cold pasta?'

'Well ... we thought you might be hungry and you might enjoy some home-cooked food,' I replied lamely.

'Why would I want cold pasta just because I'm homeless?' he asked. 'I've got fucking taste buds. Anyway, sod off, I've got a tenner and I'm off to Burger King in a bit.'

A.P.

*　　*　　*

Another time, during my university days in Bournemouth, I came out of a club at about one a.m.

one night to get some cash. I was wandering the streets looking for a cash point when I came across a female beggar with a dog, nesting in the doorway of a building society.

I sat down next to her and got chatting. She seemed a very nice person who wasn't bitter at all about her predicament, but rather relatively upbeat and reflective about it. She was quite plump and rather droll – she put me in mind of a homeless Pam Ayres. She didn't mind me sitting alongside her while she asked people for money as they passed and we carried on chatting for a while.

As usual, having had a few drinks, the more I heard of her story the more I became incensed at the indifference of society to this woman's situation, and the more I couldn't understand how I'd managed to fritter my life away up to that moment without becoming an activist for the homeless. At that moment someone came rolling down the street towards us, also looking for the cash point. As he reached us, giddy and headstrong with my new purpose in life I asked boldly, "Can you spare some change please?" He ignored me and carried on. The woman said quietly, "I'd rather you don't do that."

"Sorry," I said.

"It doesn't help," she said.

"Sorry," I said again, starting to realise quite how patronising I'd been. I was suddenly extremely uncomfortable; I felt like an idiot and wanted to get away. I gave her as much money as I had (probably about three quid) and shambled off back to the club. I never saw her again.

SEXUAL ORIENTATION

I know this isn't much of a story, but I was mortified when it happened. I'd been living in a flat in Camberwell for about two years with a whole load of people, most of whom were gay guys. We weren't exactly close friends but I liked them a lot, they were fun to be around and were very nice to me. One day I was in the kitchen and I must have been quite distracted, because one of the guys came in to show me a shirt he'd been sewing decorations onto for a party he was going to that night.

"What do you think?" he asked dubiously, giving it a critical look. "Do you think it looks gay?"

"No!" I said in my most reassuring voice. "It's fine! It looks really good!"

There was a pause. He looked at me. "No, I want it to look gay."

"Oh," I said feebly. "Yes it is. It is gay. It's really nice ..."

L.P.

I'm aware that this sounds a bit like Harry Enfield's series of sketches about the middle class dad who's afraid of offending his gay son by saying the wrong thing, but this really happened to my friend Flo. She was chatting to a girl at a party and for some reason it came as a complete surprise to her when the girl she was talking to mentioned she had a girlfriend.

As far as I know Flo has no opinion about lesbianism whatsoever, not knowing any gay women, but she was mortified when she felt a look of shock momentarily cross her face. Desperately overcompensating for this offence (which the other girl probably didn't even notice), she began insisting that she knew and liked lots of lesbians.

"I love lesbians," she kept saying, too loudly, and when she realised that this sounded a lot like the old phrase "A lot of my best friends are ...", she became so panicked that she made up a best friend called Rose, who was a lesbian. She cut off whatever the conversation had been and started talking about Rose and how well they got on together.

Then she worried that Rose sounded implausible and she went even further, making up an anecdote. "There's a funny story about me and Rose, actually," Flo said, and then realised that she would now have to improvise a funny story, which she had no idea how to do. She began to tell a tale about going for dinner with Rose to a restaurant and dragged the story out for ages with no idea how it was going to end, as the other girl stared at her. Eventually she came up with an ending where she deliberately didn't pay the bill and they ran away from the restaurant. Then she laughed much too loudly at the end of the story, which had generally made her look like a weirdo and a bit of a nasty person. By the end of it, when the girl moved on to talk to someone else, she was completely exhausted and mortified, and had said "But I love lesbians, I just love them" about six times.

J.C.

THE GYM

A few weeks ago I was in the gym changing room, getting ready for a rare "workout" session, when I realised that I had left my gym "leggings" (former pyjama bottoms) at home. I'm not into fancy gymwear so I felt undeterred. I was wearing black tights and decided that these would be a more than acceptable stand-in for the absent leggings. It wasn't until I got under the glaringly bright spot lights of the gym floor that I realised that: a) my old grey pants were more than visible under my tights, and b) I had a sizable ladder in my left leg.

"No worries," I thought, "no one will be close enough to notice." Determined to break a sweat, I launched into my workout, trying to maintain my dignity as much as possible. Having tackled the running machine and the cross trainer, I smugly settled at the arm machine for a bit of bingo wing reduction when, to my horror, a group of gym inductees eagerly gathered around my machine so that the instructor could demonstrate how to use it, close enough to see my opaque shame (thank the Lord I had at least done my bikini line).

Obviously feeling that subjecting me to this wasn't cringe worthy enough, the instructor then felt the need to point out to everyone that I was using the machine incorrectly and insisted on taking me through the correct routine, prolonging my agony.

E.H.

CLASS

It doesn't happen to me often but I remember feeling like a right middle class prat once, when I was working in my local pub. I was about 18 and the regulars were all in their 40s and 50s. I knew some of them were really quite well off and some definitely weren't, but I hadn't been working there long enough to get to know who was who and I often got them mixed up.

I was having a drink or two after time one day in the saloon bar and got chatting to one of the guys who propped it up. He was quiet, in his early or mid-50s and kept himself to himself, and when I'd noticed him (which wasn't very often) I'd not been able to tell whether he was quite respectable or a bit stupid.

Anyway, we got chatting about what I was up to and so on. I was working in my gap year before travelling and was planning to go to university the following September. Out of politeness I asked him what he did. Not really giving anything away, he said he worked in computers. How long had he done it? Since the beginning, he told me. Before the beginning in mass market terms – the mid-1970s.

"Blimey," I said, "so you were in it right at the start." And then I made a casual remark that there must be quite a lot of money made by people who were in it so early.

He gave me a cryptic look over his beer and said, "How much do you think I earn then?"

I had absolutely no idea but I began to feel incredibly awkward. It was like being asked to guess someone's age. Whichever way I went there was a chance I would offend him. I dragged it out for as long as I could, got a bit desperate and then decided to go low. Or what I thought was reasonably low for someone who'd been in probably the most massively booming industry in the world for nearly 30 years.

"Forty, fifty grand?" I said.

He didn't say anything back for a second, just looked at me and then looked down at his drink. "That's loony money," he said quietly. Then he repeated it, "That's loony money. You've got no idea." I could see from his eyes that he hadn't expected for a second I'd say anything like that much and he was really offended.

He wouldn't meet my eye. I carried on working there for another few months after that and he never spoke to me again.

H.G.

INNOCENCE

My sister is a lovely, friendly person and when she moved to south London it secretly scared the shit out of me how naïvely nice she was to everyone. She never expected anything bad might happen to her at all. So I was permanently terrified something would happen because she's such an open person.

She lived around the corner from a pizza delivery place and when she was coming back late one night from an evening out she stopped in to order a pizza. As she was ordering it she chatted cheerfully to the man who was going to deliver it to her door, and on the spur of the moment she said, "You must pop in for a cup of tea!"

She went home, put the kettle on and – this still makes my stomach turn over – changed into her nightie, ready for bed. When the pizza man came round she answered the door in said garment and, good as her word, invited him in. I don't think we can be in any doubt what he thought he was being invited in for, so he must have been puzzled, to say the least, when she appeared from the kitchen with two steaming mugs of tea in her hands, sat him down on the sofa and proceeded (at half-twelve at night) to have a nice chat, asking him polite questions about what it was like to be a pizza delivery man and offering him some of the pizza itself as she tucked into it. Then, when they'd drunk their tea, she took the cup off him, said, "It's so lovely to meet you, thanks for the delicious pizza!" and showed him to the door.

When she told me the story soon afterwards, I sat her down for a serious talk about life in a big city. Thank God she doesn't live there any more.

P.P.

FOREIGNERS

The issue of nationality can get most middle class people's knickers in a twist alright. Not my dad though, who is so relaxed in his own skin that he sits happily in Indian or Chinese restaurants and reads the menu aloud in his version of the respective accent of the country whose food he is perusing.

"Goodness gracious me!" he says loudly, as he looks around the curry house. "Rubbly, rubbly!"

If you (or I, or anyone) remonstrates with him in, say, a strained whisper, he grins manically with the look of someone who knows he's being a bit annoying in a charming sort of way but who is sure that his actions couldn't possibly be taken as offensive. What he doesn't think about is what his impression must say to the restaurant staff who surely overhear. I know how awful he sounds, but he doesn't mean to sound insulting or insensitive, he's just obliviously jolly.

Somehow my younger brother has inherited a version of this trait, which was totally unexpected by the rest of us. He's a primary school teacher, captain of the local cricket team and (unlike me) generally speaking one of those all-round good people without whom human society would simply cease to function. But he has one basic piece of faulty wiring in his brain when it comes to dealing with people who don't understand English very well, because when they ask him something he speaks English back to them in their own accent.

This has happened countless times and it's actually very funny to watch because he's totally oblivious to it. A Frenchman stops to ask him directions and, seemingly out of sympathy for their struggle with the English language, he replies as though he is similarly French and his English is just as bad as theirs. He even accompanies it with French-style hand gestures!

"Eef you ger to ther main rerd," he says, speaking loudly, "tearn left" (with violent pointing gesture to the left) "and keep ger-ing for a maisle..."

Which reminds me that, as I write, he's in Uganda for a few weeks. I hope he makes it back in one piece.

There's a dodgy alleyway opposite my flat where people get mugged. It's only about 50 yards long but it twists round twice, so you can't see the middle section from either of the roads that it connects. Even though it's between two large blocks of flats, no-one ever seems to be around when you're going down it. At night it's lit by one paltry street lamp, which gives a meagre pool of pale light – a bit like in a *film noir*, just enough for you to see how suspicious it is.

When these events took place I'd never had any trouble in the area because it's a tiny pocket of north London that's relatively safe. There are excursions into the area by the ubiquitous nearby gangs, screaming police cars to be heard every night going in different directions and – now I come to mention it – I did actually see a car-to-car shooting up the road last year. But the violence seems to stop a couple of streets back. I'm a guy in my 20s and not *completely* puny – so long as I keep my middle class mouth shut and wear my hoodie I generally feel safe. Nevertheless, when this story happened a friend had just explained to me how he'd been non-violently mugged.

"How did you manage that?" I asked.

"This guy just asked for my phone. I was miles away from anywhere, there was no way I could escape, he was way bigger than me and looked scary as hell, and he asked for it in a way that we both knew I was going to give it to him. Then he said 'Thanks mate', and went off with it." I admitted I could actually see how that would happen.

A few days later at about eight p.m. on a Saturday night, I found myself walking home through the alley, as it's a good short-cut from the bus stop. About halfway down it, two black guys stepped out in front of me and asked if they could borrow my phone. The blood rushed in my ears and I said, "Er, hang on," and kept walking fast until we were in the pool of light from the street lamp. I disconnected my headphones and asked them what they wanted. They asked if they could use my phone as there was a number they had to dial.

I ummed and ahhed, and looked awkward. They showed me their phone that had run out of credit and the number on it they had to ring in order to ask someone where they were supposed to get to tonight as they weren't from around here.

I still said nothing, just looked from my iPhone to them and back, about five times, with my mouth opening and shutting. I kept trying to think of a way of getting out of it, or of saying no, that was socially acceptable. Eventually, after a very, very long pause, it was obvious to everyone present that I was still incredibly uncomfortable about it. Finally I suggested that they give me the number and I would ring it for them.

They happily gave me the number and I phoned it but it went to voicemail – a girl's voice. I was beginning to appreciate that their manner was actually very courteous, they weren't dressed very "street" or in a way that made them look particularly shady or gang-related.

They just seemed a bit bewildered and lost. One of them offered me 50p for the call I'd made.

"No," I said, feeling more guilty by the second, and suggested to them that, seeing as their friend's phone was engaged for the time being, they could go onto the main street, find a phone box, and keep trying to get through with that 50p. They thanked me for my directions to the phone box and went on their way towards the main street. I wanted to add that jumping out on a stranger in the middle of an alley and asking for his phone was likely to encourage misunderstandings. But I was already quite wrung out by the unexpected mini-rollercoaster of fright and then guilt, and didn't want to get into a conversation about what I meant by that, so I kept my head down and walked home.

When my brother was about 12, he invited two schoolfriends home for the weekend, as they were from Malaysia and so had to spend all their weekends at school. Their names were Safi and Zaki, which weren't difficult to learn or pronounce, but for some inexplicable reason my dad started calling them Wacky and Jaffy. As if this wasn't mortifying enough, he also seemed to think they were deaf, so for the entire weekend we had to sit through Dad shouting things at them like "WACKY! WOULD YOU LIKE SOME MORE ORANGE JUICE?!' Funnily enough, they never came back.

K.D.

And now...

THE TALE THAT IS MUCH TOO HORRIBLE TO BE INCLUDED IN THE MAIN PART OF THE BOOK

This story is so infamous that it has reached the status of urban myth, which technically would have disqualified it from inclusion within this volume. But the funny thing is, it's actually true. In fact, maybe it's happened more than once – who knows? All I know is that in this instance, it really happened and is a truly depraved story that you should not read.

I'm really not joking. If you're easily offended, I'd rather you just read the rest of this book and not this bit. But if you insist, here goes ...

THE TALE OF THE WHITE SOFA

My mate Danny is a shit. He's a proper scumbag and will shag anything that moves. He's still that way now, nearly 40, with two divorces behind him. At university when I first got to know him, he was much worse. What's more, every girl he met wanted to shag him too.

A bunch of my friends were at a party shortly after university, and Danny met this girl called Alicia. He hit it off with her and fancied her like mad, and she seemed to fancy him too. He talked to her for much of the night until he persuaded her they should leave together and before you know it they were walking back to her parents' place, a mile or so away.

Both thoroughly pissed and a bit stoned – and perhaps other things besides – when they got to her house they decamped to the living room and he persuaded her that they most definitely needed to have sex. However she had a big problem – she was still a virgin, and had been saving it for someone really special. Which Danny most definitely was not. But she was high and really wanted to have sex with him. So he suggested that there was an alternative way ...

So finally, without putting too fine a point on it, they had full penetrative sex while she remained a virgin, right there on the couch. When it was done, he disengaged and they slept next to each other for a few hours before going up to bed.

The next morning Danny was woken by a scream. He went downstairs to find the girl standing in the living room. She was scrubbing madly with a cloth at a horrible brown stain on the white sofa while Danny and the loveable family dog both looked on uncomprehending.

The girl explained that the sofa was her dad's newest and most prized possession. It had been extremely expensive and it had only been delivered last week. "Look!" She pointed at the mark that Danny's dick had made. The stain wasn't going anywhere.

Danny's suggestion that they just turn the cushion over didn't help – it would be found out soon enough either way and if it had been turned over, then they would know it was her. They thought about it for ages and tried to work out a story that would be convincing and get them out of trouble. After lots of thinking, all they could come up with was that the dog had done it. The girl felt terrible for accusing her adored dog, who she'd had since she was ten, and Danny loved dogs too, but they both agreed there was no alternative. He kissed her goodbye, wished her good luck with the sofa story, and went home.

The next day the girl phoned him up, in floods of tears. He was the only person she could tell. As she had predicted, when her dad got home later that day and found out about the sofa, he'd been absolutely beside himself. When he heard it was the dog, he hadn't even waited for his temper to die down; he'd driven straight to the vet's and had the dog put down.

A.G.